TEXAS TRACKS
AND
ARTIFACTS

DO TEXAS FOSSILS INDICATE

COEXISTENCE OF MEN AND

DINOSAURS?

ROBERT F. HELFINSTINE

JERRY D. ROTH

Front Cover Photograph: Coffee Track Photo by David Lines.

Back cover drawing by Dan Lietha.
Cover designed by Kyle Hammond.

TEXAS TRACKS AND ARTIFACTS
DO TEXAS FOSSILS INDICATE COEXISTENCE OF MEN AND DINOSAURS?
Revised Edition _

R&J Publishing
1136 5th Ave. S.
Anoka, MN 55303

Library of Congress Control Number: 2007904815
ISBN 13: 978-0-615-15136-6

Printed in the United States of America at Presto Graphics Inc., Anoka, MN

TEXAS TRACKS AND ARTIFACTS

This book began as a summary report on the investigation of fossil evidence relating to the coexistence of men and dinosaurs, covering a period from 1986 to 1993. Much of the activity centered on the vicinity of Glen Rose, Texas and the Paluxy River valley where for years there have been reports of human and dinosaur tracks found in the same limestone layers. Subsequent to the 1994 date of the first printing, additional tracks have been uncovered in the Glen Rose area. Tracks discovered in prior years and in other places have also been brought to our attention.

A new section, **Supporting Evidences**, has been added to provide a broader scope of information relating to coexistence.

The evidence presented may not convince skeptics whose philosophical beliefs have already ruled out the possibility of coexistence. But we believe that the evidence as presented in the context of a Divinely created young earth and a catastrophic worldwide flood speaks for itself.

This investigation activity was initiated under the auspices of the Bible-Science Association, now Creation Moments, but the preparation and publication of this book has been the responsibility of the authors.

Robert F. Helfinstine

Jerry D. Roth

TEXAS TRACKS AND ARTIFACTS

Table of Contents

TEXAS TRACKS AND ARTIFACTS

LIST OF BLACK & WHITE ILLUSTRATIONS

LIST OF COLOR ILLUSTRATIONS

FOREWORD

Ever since Roland T. Bird, curator of the New York Museum of Natural History, visited the Paluxy River near Glen Rose, Texas back in 1928 and took out dinosaur tracks to ship back to his museum, the tracks of the Paluxy have been shrouded in mystery and controversy. The dinosaur tracks were promptly put on display, but little known is the fact that he also took out some non-dinosaurian tracks that landed in the basement of the New York museum never to see the light of day. Why? From the evolutionary viewpoint of the museum, these tracks looked too much like human footprints to be shown to the public. Thus, the quest began to unravel and investigate the mystery tracks of the Paluxy. Many, many people, some credentialed, some not, have spent hundreds and hundreds of hours digging in the limestone rocks for human tracks like those in the basement of the New York museum. This writer joined the fray back in 1982 and vigorously pursued the perfect human track yearly and sometimes twice yearly ever since. You will have to read this book to find out how successful his pursuit has been.

In this battle for the hearts and minds of men, the stakes are high if such tracks are found, for the very foundations of the evolutionary theory are destroyed if dinosaurs and humans coexisted in the past. Milne and Shafersman, evolutionists, have written "Such an occurrence would seriously disrupt conventional interpretations of the biological and geological history and would support the doctrines of creationism and catastrophism."

Bill Overn, in his foreword to the first edition to this book, was concerned with proving, in a convincing scientific manner, whether a footprint is actually human. What are some of the criteria that would lead to such a proof? We have all seen millions of footprints on a sandy beach, on a dry pavement made with wet feet, on a clean kitchen floor made by your child's muddy feet. How doubtful were you as to what kind of a creature made them? For what did you look? Were there toes? Was there a heel? Was the person flat-footed, i.e., was there an arch? Was there the typical angle across the tip of the toes? After checking out these characteristics of the human foot, you would next look for the typical trail. An adult stride varies around three feet, a child more like two. You would expect some variation to account for walking or running. Most tracks are made in a more or less straight line with small allowance for a waver here or there. There are few among us who couldn't vouch for the identification of human tracks within a very small margin of error. We all could easily rule out tracks made by dogs, cats, and bears, even gorillas or Bigfoots. In 99 out of 100 cases, you would have to want to raise a doubt as to the humanness of the track(s). I can remember a time when members of the Dallas police force were brought in to assess the character of the footprints in question. These common sense guys had no problem declaring them to be human tracks. However, if your philosophic outlook and your "scientific" background says, before you start your inquiry, that, if there is a dinosaur footprint in this limestone rock, there cannot be a human footprint there, you will be able to find all kinds of "evidence" to rule out human footprints.

In a perfect world, creationists would expect to go down to the Paluxy River bed and find perfect 10 footprints of both dinosaurs and humans because of our belief that both were created together in the beginning. There are a few things that come into play that rule out the perfect 10's. My research has led me to conclude that the sedimentary layers that are omnipresent throughout the world were laid down with the help of the semi-diurnal lunar tides acting on a global ocean called Noah's Flood. The limestone layers in question mostly precipitated out of the calcium slurry in the water composing the ocean. Therefore, one tidal assault could bring in much different slurry than the next one. This process caused much variation in the limestone from layer to layer and from place to place in the layer.

On the upper ledge of the Paluxy, there are two layers where most of the work of recent years has been done. The upper layer is very hard limestone, a fact that many men who have removed it will attest. It contains a few well-preserved dinosaur tracks. I remember seeing a particular one the first year I went to the Paluxy. It stayed there for several decades as pristine as ever until it was removed a few years ago. The lower layer, in contrast, is very soft and friable. There are many more tracks in it, both human and dinosaurian, but they do not retain the appearance they have when first excavated for very long. The dinosaurs, because of their weight, made deeper tracks and they are preserved longer. The human tracks lose their distinctiveness in a matter of months or years. Therefore, in a trail of human footprints in the lower layer, one print can be well defined while the next can be even non-descript. Such are the vagaries one faces when getting down and dirty in the Paluxy and, more or less, rule out the perfect 10 footprints.

The searches for the evidence associated with the Paluxy tracks have been well documented over the years. The most vivid in the writer's memory is the film *"Footprints in Stone"* made by Stan Taylor back in the '70's. It was a beautiful piece of work. A little later, John Morris of the Institute for Creation Research compiled the history of the quest to date in his book *" Tracking Those Incredible DINOSAURS & The People Who Knew Them. "* For many years, it was a great tribute to the fact of coexistence but, because of a stain controversy that came up in the early '80's,

Morris saw fit to pull his book from the market.

A great many other publications and presentations concerning the Paluxy tracks have been offered over the years. The authors of this book, titled *"Texas Tracks and Artifacts, "* and sub-titled "Do Texas Fossils Indicate Coexistence of Men and Dinosaurs?" presented, in 1994, an up-to-date history of not only the track controversy but also of other evidence that was found that supported the coexistence view. Since that publication date, much more work has been done to investigate the Paluxy evidence. To bring these data before the public in written form, Helfinstine and Roth have updated their work in this second edition. They have thoroughly researched the stain controversy and the overprint controversy. The Taylor Trail, with its 14 tracks in uniform stride, is given an objective reassessment. The newly rediscovered Coffee tracks are described along with the research that has been done on them. The authors have greatly expanded the section on artifacts, broadening out to recently discover worldwide evidence that lends credence to the conclusion that men and dinosaurs lived contemporaneously in the past.

As a veteran of the intriguing story of the Paluxy tracks, I recommend this book as an interesting and vital contribution to the coexistence evidence. The question in the sub-title, "Do Texas Fossils Indicate Coexistence of Men and Dinosaurs?" was given an extensive consideration by Helfinstine and Roth and deserves a confident and firm answer "Yes" from the work described in this book.

M.E.Clark
Emeritus Professor of Theoretical and Applied Mechanics and Bioengineering, University of Illinois, Urbana-Champaign, Illinois

ACKNOWLEDGEMENTS

Over the years of this investigation, numerous persons have directly and indirectly participated in the collection and analysis of information. There are several whom we wish to recognize for their part in the activities that have resulted in producing this book.

Carl E. Baugh, who shared hours of his time as well as providing photographs and details of fossil analysis which made our job of collecting pertinent data much easier.

Don R. Patton, for his continuing work in documenting tracks, for providing photographs and sketches of tracks, and for proofreading the preliminary version of this book.

John A. Watson, now deceased, for his persistence in identifying geological details and in proofreading the preliminary version of this book.

Glen Kuban, for allowing us to use some of his figures and photographs.

Bill Overn, for getting us involved in this activity and for his efforts in proofreading and setting up the text for the first edition on desktop publishing.

Fred Beierle, for letting us use several of his photos.

Paul Taylor, for allowing us to review the film *Footprints in Stone* when we first started this project.

Dan Lietha, for his artwork on the back cover.

M. E. Clark, for writing the Foreword and for his expertise in proofreading and rewording text for this second edition.

Hugh Miller for providing information on additional tracks and the material in Appendix 1 of this edition.

David Lines for his photographic input.

Alan Helfinstine for his efforts in putting the figures and text on CD ROMs.

All the participants in the scheduled dig activities whose hard work has helped to reveal the tracks and fossils found in the Paluxy River valley.

INTRODUCTION

PHILOSOPHICAL POSITION

The philosophical positions upon which the evidences gathered by the task force are evaluated include, but are not necessarily limited to, the following assumptions or presuppositions:

A young earth with the associated concepts that all living things were created in a short time period as described in the Bible, and therefore all basic types of animals and man lived at the same time.

A universal flood (Divine judgment) that produced much of the earth's sedimentary rock strata including the Cretaceous limestone found in Somervell County, Texas and the surrounding area.

A pre-flood environment that differed from the present environment. As a result of the flood and the changed environment, many species of animals became extinct, and radical changes were made in some types of plant life.

> **PRESUPPOSITIONS ARE AN IMPORTANT PART OF RESEARCH AND ANALYSIS BECAUSE THEY HAVE A SIGNIFICANT IMPACT ON CONCLUSIONS REACHED.**

Limitations in radiocarbon dating of pre-flood and early post-flood organic material because of different pre-flood and changing post-flood environment.

Rapid fossilization of buried plant and animal material.

It is recognized that, among those holding the creationist position of origins, there are differing viewpoints concerning some of the physical events that produced the sedimentary rock strata and the multitude of fossils found in them. While it is interesting to speculate, it is not the purpose of this report to define the detailed actions that produced the limestone and marl strata on which the investigation is centered. However, it is apparent that each limestone layer was laid down in a short time period, and while some were still in a semi-solid state numerous creatures left their marks in them. The question is whether or not some of those creatures were human.

EXPECTATIONS

In areas of scientific endeavor we are told that we have to learn to expect the unexpected. It is understandable that, when the Films for Christ crew under the direction of Stan Taylor uncovered the trail of footprints that became known as the Taylor Trail, they assumed their expectations of finding human-like footprint depressions in the hardened limestone were fulfilled. The natural tendency, when examining new information, is to look for explanations that relate to what is already known. Also, expectations control perception, and details which may seem ambiguous or irrelevant are often overlooked. Stan Taylor's expectations were based on first hand witnesses that testified of seeing detailed human-like tracks in the Paluxy limestone. The review of the Taylor Trail evidence by qualified scientific personnel and the general concurrence that the tracks appeared to be human-like added support to their conclusions.

It was the unexpected revelation that previously observed but not fully defined details of the Taylor Trail now showed definite tridactyl (three toed) characteristics. This resulted in renewed examination of the total evidence for the coexistence of man and dinosaurs in the Paluxy area.

As one who at first had been skeptical of the man-like tracks when I learned about them some years ago, I had accepted the evidence of "expert observers", and in conjunction with other archeological and geological evidences, I had no doubt that men and dinosaurs could leave tracks in a layer of fast hardening limestone mud. Having never seen the Paluxy River first hand when the independent task force was formed, I went there for the first time in April of 1986 with certain expectations based on films, photographs, slides and video coverage of some previous excavation activities. I understood, along with other task force members, that gathering first hand scientific evidence to solve this controversial issue was not going to be an easy task. New evidence still had to be discovered since existing evidence was in many instances so badly eroded that it was no longer relevant for the present investigation. Our expectations were tempered by our established criteria that any new evidence had to be subjected to detail examination and thoroughly documented.

For those who have differing philosophical views and presuppositions, it is apparent that their expectations will not coincide with ours. Evidence in conflict with presuppositions, whether ours or others with opposing views, requires some thinking processes as presuppositions are re-evaluated. All data must be included in the final explanation of the past in to which we are looking.

RESULTS

It has taken longer than anticipated to come to the present position of preparing a report on our findings. There have been moments of excitement followed by months of analysis and waiting for detailed results. Some evidence is still being analyzed. But much has been learned, and hopefully new information has been established that will serve as a basis for understanding this complex geological formation and its varied fossil evidences.

R. F. Helfinstine
Task Force Leader

Introduction Addendum -2006

It has been 13 years since the first printing of Texas Tracks and Artifacts. The search for tracks in the Paluxy River valley continues. Additional tracks and trails have been uncovered, and some earlier-found tracks have revealed more details. Other tracks have deteriorated due to the eroding effects of flowing water and sand particles, especially abrasive during times of high water.

Tracks found in other locations have added to the list of evidences showing that man lived in the theoretical age of dinosaurs. Some rock strata containing tracks are supposedly much older than the Cretaceous limestone found in the Paluxy valley. These findings further support our presupposition that much of the sedimentary rock strata found in the geologic column were produced over a brief period of time as the result of the Biblical global flood.

One of the benefits of the ongoing search for dinosaur fossils, whether in the Paluxy River valley or in other locations, is the educational benefit to the students that are taking part in excavation activities.

Supporting evidence for the coexistence of men and dinosaurs has been added at the end of this book. This includes some significant artwork and historical references.

Part I
HISTORICAL DEVELOPMENT

This section outlines the investigation of the tracks and related finds in a semi-chronological manner.

PAST HISTORY OF PALUXY TRACK FINDS

Track Types

Dinosaur tracks of the type found in the Glen Rose area are found in a number of locations in Texas. One area of exposed tracks that John Watson investigated is along the Lampasas River near Rumly. Another site is along the South San Gabriel River near Leander, Texas.

In 1938 Roland T. Bird of the American Museum of Natural History in New York brought attention to dinosaur tracks when he had some tracks removed and placed on exhibit at the museum.

The most common track type in the Glen Rose area is the large three-toed, bird-like impression belonging to the Acrocanthosaurus, a two-legged carnosaur belonging to the same group as the larger Tyrannosaurus rex.

The second type of track was finally identified in 1985 as probably belonging to an Iguanodon, a two-legged ornithopod. The bird-like tracks are not as large as those of the Acrocanthosaurus. The toes are stubby and the heel is more rounded.

A third category of tracks belongs to a four-legged sauropod named Pleurocoelus. The front foot track impression is similar to that of a horse hoof, but the hind feet make an oval impression with distinct indentations of its four toes. Figure 48 shows a comparison of these tracks. (Ref: Dinosaur Valley State Park bulletin, 1998) Non-dinosaur tracks that have been found in the Glen Rose area rock strata include cat tracks, bear tracks and human-like tracks (homo sapiens). Evolutionists and some long-age creationists dispute these types of tracks because of their philosophical beliefs.

Track Finders

Reports of finding both human and dinosaur fossil tracks, technically known as ichnofossils, in the limestone strata of the Paluxy River valley goes back to the early 1900s. Interviews with local residents who had seen some of the early tracks were included in the film *Footprints in Stone* by Stan Taylor and Films for Christ. Human-like tracks were reported to have been removed from the riverbed and sold, but because of no formal documentation of the removals, the few removed tracks that are still available for examination are looked at with scepticism since there were also reports of tracks having been carved. Since the dinosaur tracks were in more demand for selling, the human-like tracks, whether genuine or carved, were not of as much interest in the early days. Some early photographs of excavations of dinosaur prints are still available.

Because of the many dinosaur tracks along the Paluxy River, it was a natural location for the study of dinosaurs. Colleges and universities scheduled field trips to the location to study and map trails, and several museums removed sections of dinosaur tracks for display.

It wasn't until Stan Taylor began filming *Footprints in Stone* that more detailed documentation of tracks and track excavation was done. His interest had been aroused by work done by Dr. Clifford Burdick and reported in The *Genesis Flood* by John Whitcomb and Henry Morris. In his film, Stan Taylor showed a number of close-up views of human-like prints from the Dinosaur Valley State Park ledge that were already exposed at the time of his investigation, but specific locations were not identified. Much of the film activity relating to the Taylor Trail did not show close up views of the exposed tracks.

At the time of the filming, scientists who observed the Taylor Trail in 1970 were photographed giving their comments about the nature of the footprints. These comments were included in the Paluxy documentary film *Footprints in Stone*. Pertinent comments are included in the following paragraphs.

Dr. Douglas Block, professor of geology, Rock Valley College, Rockford, Illinois.
"If not made by man, we don't know what kind of animal produced them"

He later wrote to John Morris that the tracks were completely human. (Morris, John, 1980, p. 35)

Dr. Harold Slusher, Assistant professor of physics, Univ. of Texas, El Paso.
His comments were that some of the tracks showed good detail, toes, instep, and general shape of a foot.

Dr. Clifford Burdick, consulting geologist, Tucson, Arizona.
He was convinced that there was still enough of the track to identify it as a human footprint, even though erosion had weathered some of the details.

Dr. Paul Wright, professor emeritus of geology, Wheaton College, Illinois.
He stated that the tracks were made by an animal of some kind. If it were not for the Cretaceous limestone, they would be considered human.

Dr. Gerald H. Haddock, Geology professor, Wheaton College.
He doubted that they were man tracks even though they looked like man tracks.

Dr. Henry Morris, hydrologist, Director of Institute for Creation Research (ICR).
He stated that we know of no animal, past or present, that could have made the tracks except man.

It should be noted that opinions expressed at that time are not necessarily the present opinions of these individuals.

Apparently few detailed drawings of the track features were made when the Taylor Trail was first exposed, but Stan Taylor's notes and sketch of the trail show erratic external marks on several of the prints with the comment "apparent splash mark or erosion" written by it. Figure 1 is a reproduction of one of his note pages with a mid-1970s photo of part of the trail included. Now, due to disclosure of additional information, we recognize these markings as partially exposed dinosaur track features. Stan Taylor also made a cast of the +1 human-like print. From a photo of a reproduction of the original cast an approximate print outline has been reproduced and is shown in Figure 2. The anterior of the print was very distinct in the photo. Although individual toe details did not show, the distinct slope of the toe outline is characteristic of a human foot. If this type of detail is indicative of what was observed in other prints when they were first uncovered, it is understandable that the tracks would be identified as human. But this is probably not the case. The impressions in the trail were called giant man tracks although the longest measurement listed on Stan's notes is 16 inches.

Dr. Cecil Dougherty moved to Glen Rose, Texas in the 1960s and became interested in the giant tracks found in the Paluxy River bed. The report of his activities and discoveries is contained in the booklet *Valley of the Giants*. This has gone through seven editions as he has updated it a number of times. The Dougherty Trail of human-like tracks was found in 1971. Not all of his track finds have been accepted as being authentic.

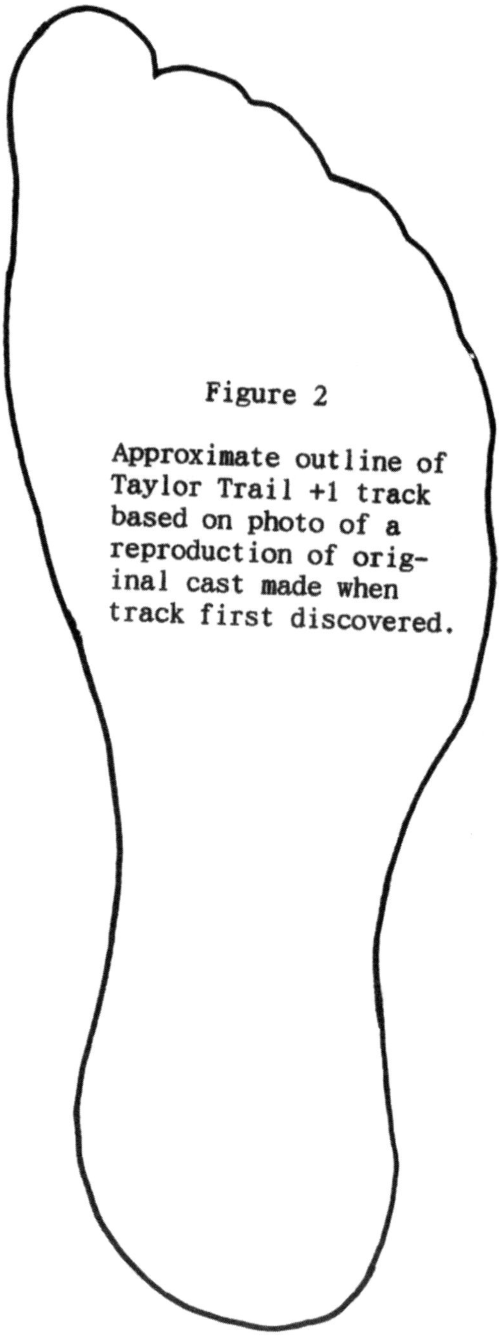

Fred Beierle also investigated the man-like tracks in the Paluxy valley. He published the booklet *Giant Man Tracks* in 1974 that contains a number of pictures of both dinosaur and human-like tracks. In 1980 he published a second book, *Man, Dinosaur and History*. In it he reported the find by professor Wilbur Fields of a burned tree branch that was buried in the limestone but had been exposed by the erosion effects of the river. Radio carbon dating of a sample gave a radiometric date of 12,800 +/- 200-radiometric years, much younger than the assumed date of the Cretaceous limestone. (Beierle, Frederic, 1979, p. 87; 1980, pp7,8, 69-75)

Wilbur Fields, professor of archaeology and history at Ozark Bible College, did considerable mapping of trails and excavation sites. He also provided the numbering sequences for various trails including the Taylor trail. In 1978 he published the preliminary report *Paluxy River Explorations* that included photographic documentation of many dinosaur and human-like trails as well as trail diagrams.

Dr. John Morris of ICR did detailed studies in the late 1970s of the Paluxy River area and the various sites of reported man tracks. His results are in the 1980 book *Tracking Those Incredible DINOSAURS & the People Who Knew Them*.

Glen Kuban has done extensive research on tracks and markings in the Paluxy River area from 1980 to the present. He and his co-workers have photographed and made detailed measurements of known trails and have mapped several Paluxy sites including the Taylor site. Kuban has published articles on the results of his investigation and analysis of tracks, some of which are referenced in sections of this report. One of his more significant articles, printed in the Spring/ Summer edition of *Origins Research*, is

Figure 2

Approximate outline of Taylor Trail +1 track based on photo of a reproduction of original cast made when track first discovered.

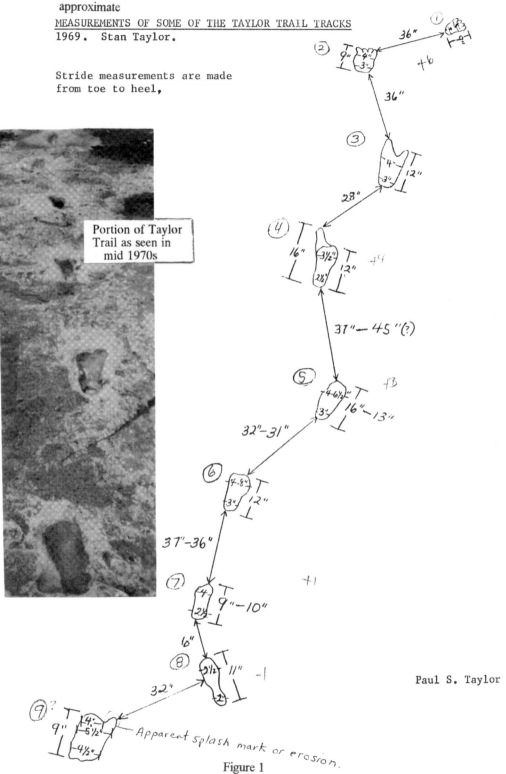

approximate

MEASUREMENTS OF SOME OF THE TAYLOR TRAIL TRACKS
1969. Stan Taylor.

Stride measurements are made
from toe to heel,

Portion of Taylor
Trail as seen in
mid 1970s

Paul S. Taylor

Apparent splash mark or erosion.

Figure 1

Copy of Stan Taylor's notes with 1970s photo of Taylor Trail. Picture covers
tracks –3 to +3.

(Stan's drawing is not to scale. Note that trail sequence in photo is more in
straight line than shown in sketch.

The Taylor Site "man tracks". This article provides an explanation of how elongate dinosaur tracks were probably made.

The most recent activities in uncovering tracks along the Paluxy River began in 1982 when Carl Baugh went to Glen Rose in search of tracks. Digging on the McFall property upstream from where others had been digging and on rock strata above normal river levels, he found many dinosaur and some human-like prints. He has been assisted in his excavation activities at different times by individuals from all types of backgrounds, varying from students, schoolteachers and pastors to technical experts with advanced degrees and impeccable credentials. This activity has continued to the present time, and has resulted in the construction of a museum to display many of the prints and other evidences found in the area as well as fossils and artifacts from other locations.

Also in recent years, Dr. John DeVilbiss has done some excavation work at the Kerr site across the river from the McFall site, and the Hugh Miller team has excavated on the McFall site.

Reaction of the Secular Community

There have been mixed opinions about the identification of the different tracks found along the Paluxy River. The different dinosaur tracks have not caused much concern about their authenticity, but the prints that resemble human footprints have been dismissed as carvings or erosion marks by some but strongly supported as genuine human prints by others. Local residents, who have found some of the better quality human-like prints, have been supportive of the claim of genuine human origin in spite of the large size of many tracks.

Some geologists, paleontologists and other scientifically trained individuals have dismissed the human-like footprints on philosophical grounds since the Cretaceous limestone in which they are found is theoretically too old according to the evolutionary model to have human or other mammal type evidence in it.

Reaction of Creationists

Many of the Creationists who became aware of the human-like tracks found along the Paluxy River were quick to recognize the significance of their association with dinosaur tracks. The large size of many of the tracks caused some skepticism, but the Bible was quite clear in its statements that in those days giants lived on the earth (Gen. 6:4). Many relied on the word of "expert witnesses" who had seen the tracks or on the written reports of the tracks. Those who traveled to Texas to see the tracks were often disappointed if they only went to the State park, since the official position of park personnel was that no human-like tracks existed in the park. Others who knew of the track locations were also disappointed at times because of the unpredictable nature of the river level. Flash flooding occurs at times when there are local heavy rainstorms, and when the river is high most of the tracks are covered. Even at normal river levels many tracks are under water, and only during extended dry spells does the river drop to a level where the Taylor trail is easily observed.

Some who consider themselves creationists do not hold to a "young earth" position and so do not even accept the idea that men and dinosaurs lived at the same time, much less accept track evidence as indication of their coexistence. Others are looking for better quality evidence and have been critical of the claims made in the past.

Excavation in recent years of tracks on the ledge above the normal river level caused renewed interest among creationists. Here, the limestone is mixed with clay (illite) resulting in a very friable matrix. The rapid erosion of these tracks when they are exposed to the sun and rain left others doubtful because all they could see were shallow depressions within a few months of excavation. State laws prohibited the removal of tracks, even for analysis.

In general, the variety of locations that showed human-like tracks gave many creationists a high level of confidence in the authenticity of the coexistence of humans and dinosaurs.

BEGINNING OF RECENT CONTROVERSY

There has been controversy over man-like tracks found in the Glen Rose area and other locations dating back to the 1950s and possibly before. The controversy renews each time a publication comes out with claims of new tracks. It was renewed when the film *Footprints in Stone* was released.

Questions About Track Identification

In 1980, Glen Kuban had gone to Glen Rose hoping to find human tracks with plans to document whatever he found. His stated main reason in personal correspondence was to "not only to document the markings, but also to *determine exactly what they were.* That is, I was not only interested in whether they were human or not, but if they were not human, what they really were, and how they were formed". In his observations and documentation of the Taylor trail, he found dinosaur digit impressions that caused him to discount any human-like features (Kuban, Glen J., 1986). He concluded that the Taylor trail was a series of elongate, metatarsal dinosaur tracks before any coloration features were identified. Kuban continued his investigations and documentation of the Taylor site and other sites on an annual basis.

The river bed dried up in 1984 and allowed

detailed observations of the Taylor site and other areas of the river bed. It was during this time that Kuban concluded that color and texture defined some prints more precisely than track depressions and mud push-up. While he and Ron Hastings cleared more track areas, previously undocumented tracks were identified by the color distinction where there was only slight topographic relief in the limestone (Kuban, Glen J., 1986). This helped them to fill in missing tracks from some trails. At this time of low water, others besides Kuban and Hastings took pictures of the tracks in which the color distinction clearly showed dinosaur features as shown in Figure C-1.

In 1984 ICR personnel were invited by Kuban to see the new features observed at the Taylor site and other areas including those of Carl Baugh's, but it wasn't until October 1985 that John Morris, Paul Taylor, Mrs. Marian Taylor and others who helped make the film Footprints in Stone visited the site. At that time there was some water flowing over the trail but the coloration markings showed clearly (Hastings, Ron J., 1988). The dinosaurian nature of the tracks was acknowledged by Morris and Taylor.

One of the initial reactions of Morris, and echoed by others, was that the prints in the Taylor Trail may have been tampered with, but since some of the markings could be seen in the *Footprints in Stone* film, this did not seem likely.

A question that was raised about the Taylor tracks was, how could so many qualified observers take part in the excavation and examination of the tracks and not notice the characteristics that were now causing embarrassment to those who made and promoted the film? With few detailed photographs or drawings of individual prints made at the time of their discovery, it was hard to second-guess the appearance of the tracks at that time. But dinosaurian impression and coloration features have been found in early documentation. Erosion has removed much of the mud push-up that was present when the tracks were first uncovered. But erosion has also revealed information that was not visible initially. Tracks -3B and -3C could not be detected when Wilbur Fields gave numbers to the tracks, hence the addition of the B and C designations. But because of the controversy, Films for Christ withdrew the film *Footprints in Stone* from circulation.

Two articles were published about the time the controversy was being renewed. John R. Cole's article *Did humans and dinosaurs live together in Texas?-NO!* was responded to by Dr. John W. DeVilbiss in the article *Did humans and dinosaurs live together in Texas?-MAYBE.* (Origins Research, Vol. 6, No.2) Creationists who supported the coexistence concept were put on the defensive. Since many had never seen the evidence first-hand and were relying on the reports of the few who had been directly involved, they were unsure of their position when some of the supporters of human-like tracks backed down from their original position. The following statement from an article by Dr. John Morris of ICR in the January 1986 Impact (No.151) seemed to eliminate nearly all known human-like tracks as evidence for coexistence of dinosaurs and men.

> "In view of these developments, none of the four trails at the Taylor site can today be regarded as unquestionably of human origin. The Taylor Trail appears, obviously, dinosaurian, as do two prints thought to be in the Turnage Trail. The Giant Trail has what appear to be dinosaur prints leading toward it, and some of the Ryals tracks seem to be developing claw features, also.

> "Trails and prints everywhere along the Paluxy, while contributive to the original interpretation, may be insufficient to stand alone. Erosion has further deteriorated the once-interesting prints on the park ledge, but they are still recognizable. At the Dougherty site, no hints of the important Cherry Trail and Morris prints remain. The various controversial prints labeled as human by Carl Baugh in recent years are of uncertain origin, and at best are not comparable in quality to prints at the sites above, thereby providing no support for the original position."

The Impact article drew mixed responses. Not all agreed with the conclusions stated in the article, and some thought that ICR had gone too far in their abandoning all the human-like claims. Others familiar with the Taylor site thought that Morris had not gone far enough. Glen Kuban responded to the **Impact** article in an *Origins Research* article **"Review of ICR Impact Article 151"**. The change in appearance certainly required some explanation, but not a wholesale renouncement of original conclusions before a thorough investigation of the matter. Because of ICR's stature in the field of creationism, their statements had a significant effect on creationists who have never seen the evidence.

A statement from an article by Films for Christ in the Spring/Summer 1986 issue of *Origins Research* relates their concern about claims for the Taylor Trail.

> "There is no question that the 'human-like' tracks excavated by Mr. Taylor are real impressions - not carved

hoaxes or erosion marks, as numerous evolutionists have long charged without first-hand examination. It is certain that no hoax or fabrication of evidence was involved in the original identification of `human-like' tracks excavated by Taylor. Although new findings indicate the early research was not as thorough as we now would wish (in light of new data), his work remains an impressive effort, showing good technique and logic. His field work and documentation have always been open to public evaluation by the scientific community. His work was publicly evaluated by several scientists. *Footprints in Stone* was finally released and kept in distribution on the strength of their positive affirmations combined with a logical interpretation of then available data.

"Caution Advised

"Based on research which is still incomplete, it would be hasty to discredit all earlier conclusions of able researchers and Glen Rose residents regarding the identification of certain tracks as `human' or `human-like.' However, the new evidence at hand certainly requires a re-evaluation and possible re-interpretation of all the data gathered. We highly recommend that no one represent any of the Paluxy tracks as proven evidence of human existence during the Cretaceous until final, reliable conclusions can be reached regarding new and old data."

One important fact emerged from the controversy. Any further excavation work and significant discoveries had to be documented in such a way that there would be no question about what was found, and the details of the find, especially tracks, would be preserved even though erosion could quickly change the actual features.

During the investigation of the Taylor Trail and the associated coloration marks, additional dinosaur tracks were discovered which consisted only of coloration areas in the limestone. These well-defined tracks indicated that additional animal activity had taken place in a relatively short time to produce all the tracks now documented in a limited area. A map of the Taylor site is shown in Figure 3. This map denotes several of the main dinosaur trails in this area although there are other tracks not shown. The Taylor trail has been darkened for easy identification. A map of the Paluxy River investigation area is shown in Figure 4, indicating the relative locations of the Taylor site, the McFall site, Dinosaur Valley State Park and the Creation Evidence Museum. To help understand the physical profile of the area, a sketch of the sedimentary rock layers is shown in Figure 5. Excavation activities have primarily been in the Glen Rose formation.

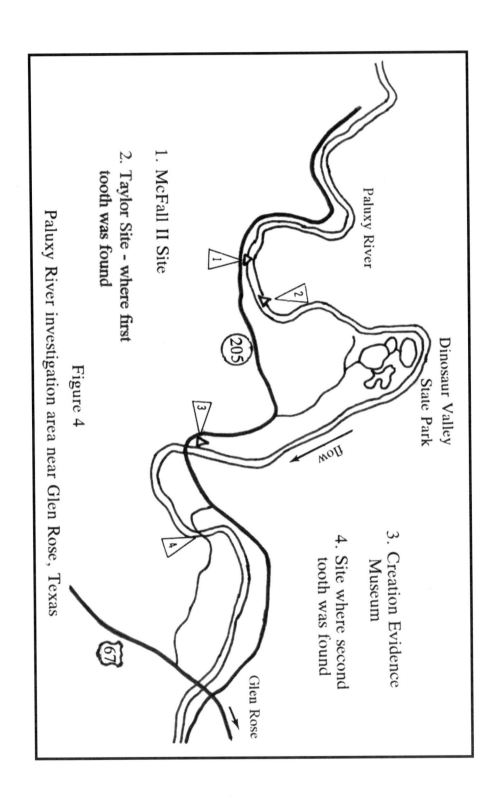

1. McFall II Site

2. Taylor Site - where first tooth was found

3. Creation Evidence Museum

4. Site where second tooth was found

Figure 4

Paluxy River investigation area near Glen Rose, Texas

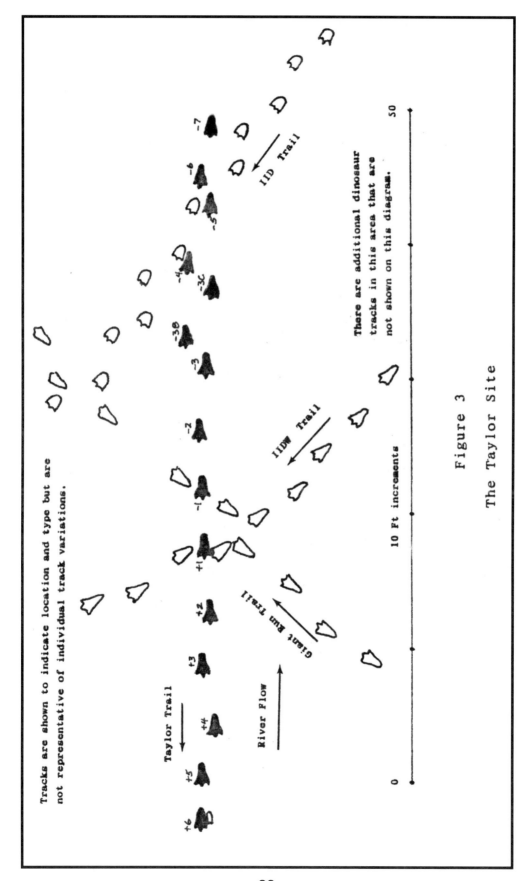

Figure 3

The Taylor Site

FORMATION OF THE TASK FORCE

Objective

Because the Bible-Science Association had published reports on the Paluxy tracks and had actively supported, along with a number of its branch chapters, the promotion of the film *Footprints in Stone*, it was determined that a position must be taken as a result of the controversy. This position must be based primarily on facts and verified evidence. The wealth of historical evidence gathered by qualified scientific observers in the past and supported by public observers, while not subject to scientific analysis because of the transient nature of much of the evidence, does provide a background of information that cannot be ignored.

W. M. Overn, then with the Bible-Science Association, announced the formation of the Task Force in early 1986. Its stated purpose was "to gather the most accurate scientific information possible on the present evidence for the alleged human footprints on the Paluxy". A second purpose was to establish the most appropriate position for the Bible-Science Association and other creationist organizations to take in regard to the whole subject of human evidence in conjunction with dinosaurs.

Original Task Force members included
  Paul Bartz, BSA staff coordinator
  Robert Helfinstine, task force leader
  Al Heitkamp, chemistry leader
  Jerry Roth, analysis team

Both Bill Overn and Jerry Roth had been involved in excavation activities along the Paluxy River in December 1983 so there was some familiarity with the area by persons in the task force. During the December 1983 excavation, several dinosaur tracks were uncovered.

Since others were also doing research in the human/dinosaur area, contact was made with some of them to establish the possibility of information exchange. This was done to speed up the data acquisition process and to keep costs to a reasonable level.
Contact was made with:
  Dr. John Morris of ICR
  Dr. John W. DeVilbiss of Office of Research on Origins.
  Glen J. Kuban, an independent researcher.
  Dr. Carl Baugh of Creation Evidence Museum.
  Dr. Ron Hastings, physicist.
  Don R. Patton, geologist.

Initial Collection of Information

In this document, a number of fossil types will be described. See page 119 for a brief description of fossils.

Information, which was collected by the task force to start the investigation, consisted of personal letters, newspaper articles, brochures, photographs and other miscellaneous items. Detailed photos, taken at the time of the discovery of the trail, were sought, but few could be found. As the investigation progressed, the film *Footprints in Stone* was reviewed, thanks to Paul Taylor of Films for Christ. Since this film was at the center of the controversy, it was necessary to verify the reported allegations that it showed the reptilian print pattern in a view of the Taylor trail. A brief segment of the film lasting only several seconds showed the color pattern extending from the front of the track depression, but the film had to be stopped to see it clearly.

The book *Tracking Those Incredible Dinosaurs and the People Who Knew Them* by Dr. John Morris was also reviewed since it dealt with the Taylor Trail and other tracks.

Because the controversy brought up the

Sketch based on information from
<u>Roadside Geology of Texas</u>, 1991
by Darwin Spearing

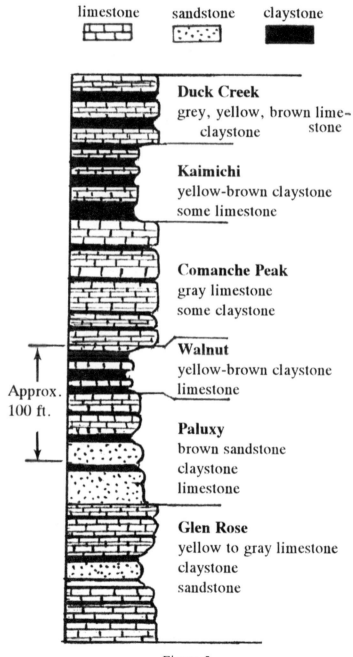

limestone   sandstone   claystone

Duck Creek
grey, yellow, brown lime-
claystone   stone

Kaimichi
yellow-brown claystone
some limestone

Comanche Peak
gray limestone
some claystone

Walnut
yellow-brown claystone
limestone

Paluxy
brown sandstone
claystone
limestone

Glen Rose
yellow to gray limestone
claystone
sandstone

Approx.
100 ft.

Figure 5

Lower Cretaceous rock layers
Vicinity of Dinosaur Valley State Park

question of possible track staining for the purpose of altering their appearance, much of the early investigation dealt with finding out about staining and what the tracks in question actually looked like.

On April 21 and 22, 1986 the task force leader visited Glen Rose, Texas to see first hand what the area looked like, and also to determine what the stained prints looked like. It was learned at that time that the tracks in question were primarily those of the Taylor trail, although the Turnage and Ryals trails were also being questioned. Led by Dr. Carl Baugh, director of the Creation Evidence Museum, and accompanied by Bill Ellis, a geologist from San Antonio, the three went to the site of the Taylor trail. It was covered with about ten inches of water at that time, but since the water was clear it did not hamper observations. Three sequential tracks of the Taylor Trail were observed near some dinosaur tracks of the IIDW trail. After removing a thin layer of silt from two of the tracks, the coloring in the rock and the questionable `stain' outlines were quite clear. Also, by feeling one of the tracks, it was determined that mud push-up around the depression did not necessarily follow the color outline of the dinosaur track. This led to speculation of superimposed tracks, also known as overprinting, where a secondary human-like impression is located within the outline of the dinosaur track, but there was not enough evidence obtained at that time to make a positive determination. Further investigation was warranted, but since the first visit was primarily concerned with gathering evidence on staining and coloration marks, those activities were given the highest priority.

General observations of the rock layers at the Taylor site and at other locations indicated that there is color at or near the surface, some of which is the same color as the reported stain area. The coloring in the rock is not all the same, varying from a yellow-orange to red to almost maroon in some places. Where the rock is not worn, the colored layer is covered with a thin, light colored calcite layer. Comments made by the observers were that one would not have to stain the rock to make alterations in track appearance. Removing the thin calcite layer to expose the colored layer would achieve the same result and would look more natural because one would not have to match the rock color with a staining agent.

Rock color characteristics are shown in Figure 6. The surface color feature appears to be caused by penetration into the limestone by iron oxide. The broken rock layers along the Paluxy River show this feature.

Rock samples from loose pieces of the second limestone layer were taken at the McFall site upstream from the Taylor trail for the purpose of making a chemical analysis of the colored outer layer of the rock to compare with the analysis of the interior of the rock. The results are provided in the Analysis section.

Photographic reprints of some of the Taylor trail and some dinosaur tracks taken in 1984 when the river was dry were examined. It was noted that some of these pictures show the stain marks quite clearly. Figure C-1 shows the color pattern in one of the Taylor

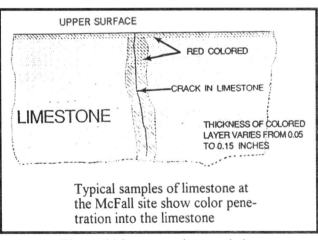

Typical samples of limestone at the McFall site show color penetration into the limestone

Figure 6 Limestone characteristics

trail tracks.

The area where Dr. Carl Baugh had been excavating on the McFall site was also examined. While many tracks of dinosaurs were still visible, the alleged human tracks were eroded to rounded depressions in the rock layer. Some of the depressions were isolated, that is, they were not a part of a sequence. Information obtained from Dr. Baugh indicated that there were no details on these isolated depressions to identify them as human-like tracks. It was only that they were found in the vicinity of trails of human-like tracks. The initial reaction was to consider these as something other than human tracks, but exactly what was not clear at the time.

More Color Investigation

Dr. John Morris and John Mackay visited the Paluxy River area in 1986 and obtained core samples from the Taylor trail and from adjacent dinosaur prints. In June of 1986 Dr. John Morris sent a preliminary evaluation of the cores to the Task Force. The task force leader visited ICR in October 1986 while on a trip to California and had a chance to see these core samples and Dr. John Morris' notes. The cores were identified as to location and had been sawed in two for examination. They were observed in a dry condition under artificial light. No definite conclusions could be reached from this initial examination. Figure 7 is a sketch of some of the details.

Glen Kuban and Ron Hastings later removed core samples from this same area. Colored photographs of his cores were sent to the task force along with some written information. Those photographs, taken when the cores were wet, clearly show the difference between the track coloration and the basic limestone rock. The print area has evidently been infilled after the tracks were made. Difference in composition between the track and the undisturbed limestone evidently allow the track to hold more iron oxide and show a color contrast. It was later learned that exposure to sunlight apparently enhances the color distinction.

In the process of investigating the Paluxy area, photographs, cores, rock analysis results, etc., it was initially thought that the

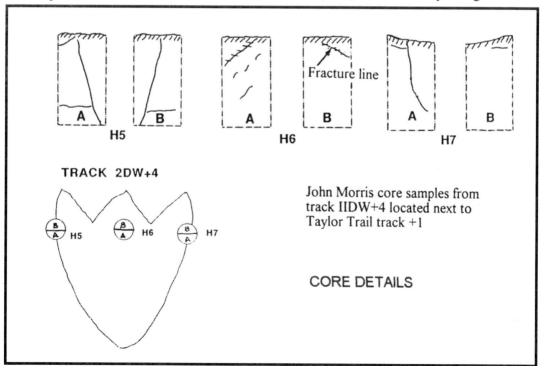

Figure 7

basic Taylor trail may not be a trail of human foot prints, but the recorded observations of those who saw it before erosion changed the features as originally exposed by Stan Taylor required additional explanation. Early observers were convinced that the track features were sufficiently human-like to warrant their acceptance of them as such. What had changed?

The superimposed track concept was still being considered. But without detailed evidence, either from the time of the trail discovery or from new information, there was no way to substantiate the hypothesis. Also, the vast number of previous tracks from other sites identified as being "human" could not be overlooked. Since most of these older tracks were eroded too badly to identify or else were removed from the limestone without documentation (such as the Burdick track at the Creation Evidence Museum), it was concluded that something more significant than what was already available was needed to verify human and dinosaur coexistence. What was hoped for was a definite human artifact or human skeletal remains in undisputable association with the dinosaur tracks. Considering the vast area over which the dinosaurs and possible humans were roaming, it was like looking for a needle in a haystack, but only having a small part available for observation. However, the search for new tracks and other evidence continued.

Activities During the Investigation Period

More Tracks

In October 1986, Dr. John DeVilbiss, a geophysicist from California, along with Dr. Carl Baugh excavated a good sixteen-inch human-like footprint on the Kerr site located across the river from the McFall II site. This track appeared to be the beginning of another trail. The track was later defaced with chisel marks by parties unknown so that specific details were not visible. The distinction between natural depressions and chisel marks was quite evident.

In January 1987, M. E. Clark, professor from the Univ. of Illinois, was excavating at the McFall II site with Dr. Baugh. They uncovered three human-like footprints in the second limestone layer (from top), one of which had good detail and is hereafter referred to as the Clark print. These were adjacent to and appeared to be crossing a trail of three-toed dinosaur tracks. Since it was not possible for any of the task force members to go to Texas at that time, the tracks were kept covered with sandbags to preserve them from the elements. The task force leader observed them several months later. A photograph of the Clark print is shown in Figure C-10 with professor Wilbur Fields, and an enlargement is shown in Figure C-11.

Tooth Find

An archeological dig sponsored by the Creation Evidence Museum was scheduled for the week of June 15-19, 1987. The first day's activities consisted of cleaning up flood debris from the previous week of high water and of removing a large piece of limestone rock from the top layer. This was adjacent to the dinosaur trail and the Clark footprint. On the second day Dr. Baugh began removing the clay marl that was underneath the rock removed the previous day. At 12:05 PM Dr. Baugh uncovered a tooth in the marl about three inches above the second limestone layer. It was black in color and had no root attached. Dr. Baugh tentatively identified it as a human deciduous (child's) incisor because of its shape and size. Philip Isett, soil scientist from West Texas State University, and Don Patton, geologist from Dallas, both certified that the marl in which the tooth was found was an undisturbed layer. Other witnesses to the tooth find were Joe and Melinda Crews, Rick Tingle, Bob Helfinstine and Mark Ludy.

After documenting the tooth find, additional excavation work was done on Tuesday and

Wednesday. A turtle bone, also black in color, was found near where the tooth was found. Fossil plant remains were found within inches of where the tooth was found. These were later identified as part of the root structure of a lepidodendron, a fossil fern tree, found several feet away.

On Thursday morning, June 18, Dr. James Addison, a dentist from Dallas, arrived to examine the tooth. He immediately identified it as an upper right central incisor, deciduous tooth, a child's tooth. After measuring the tooth he stated that it was within the range of modern teeth, although on the large side of the range. Additional photographs were made at that time. Geologist Don Patton returned later that evening from Dallas with enlargements of the tooth photos. He had shown the photos to two other dentists who had also identified it as a human tooth. Figures C-39 and C-40 show the lingual (tongue side) and labial (lip side) views respectively of the tooth.

Excavation work continued on Friday morning. This resulted in the discovery of a second turtle bone. We had been expecting to find another human footprint extending back from the trail that included the Clark print, but this was not found.

At a news conference a week later when the discovery was announced to the public, orthopedic surgeon Kenneth Hogan, DMD, of Fort Smith, Arkansas verified the identification made earlier by Dr. Addison.

Also present was Swiss organic chemist A.E. Wilder-Smith, Ph. D. The Somervell Sun newspaper carried the headlines "Creation Evidence Confirmed" in its weekly publication. Evolutionists were quick to declare the tooth an incisor from an extinct fossil fish, a pycnodont, since a number of their teeth have been found in the area.

The tooth was initially sent to Dr. David Menton, a microscopic anatomist at Washington University Medical School in St. Louis, MO., for analysis. Later it was sent to Dr. James McIntosh, professor of anatomy and histology at Baylor School of Dentistry in Dallas, for further analysis.

Lepidodendron Found

In December 1987 between Christmas and New Years, additional digging was done adjacent to where the tooth was found, again looking for a continuation of the trail in which the Clark print was found. This dig activity was in conjunction with a Genesis Institute seminar. Excavation was done a few feet downstream from the site excavated in June, and a coalified section of the root of a "lepidodendron" was found. Identification of the lepidodendron was made by Michael Rhinehart who had the identification confirmed by the curator emeritus of the Gilcrest Museum of Natural History in Oklahoma City. This is a fern tree type plant that grew to heights of 60 to 100 feet. It is listed as a Permian type species that has never before been reported being found in

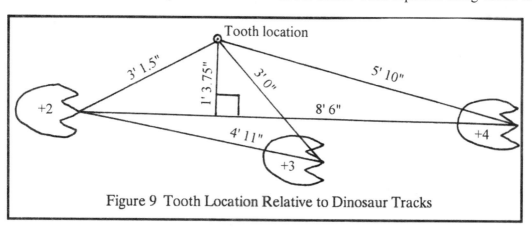

Figure 9 Tooth Location Relative to Dinosaur Tracks

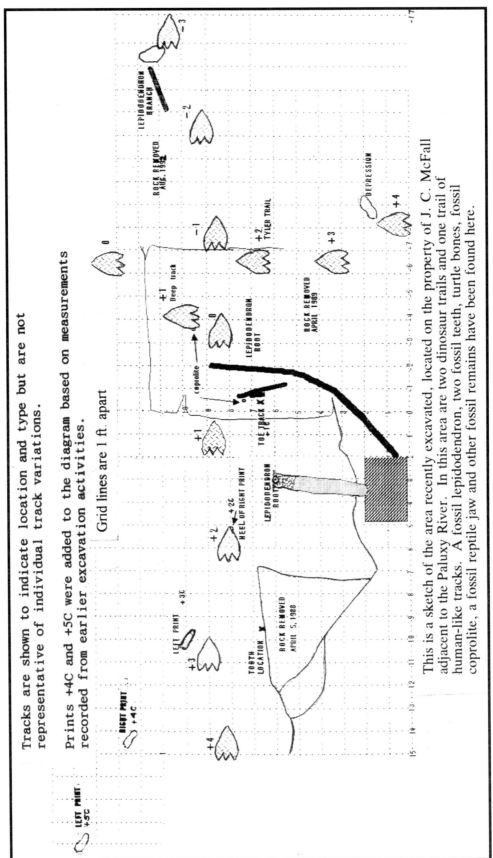

Tracks are shown to indicate location and type but are not representative of individual track variations.

Prints +4C and +5C were added to the diagram based on measurements recorded from earlier excavation activities.

Grid lines are 1 ft. apart

Figure 8, Mc Fall II Site.

This is a sketch of the area recently excavated, located on the property of J. C. McFall adjacent to the Paluxy River. In this area are two dinosaur trails and one trail of human-like tracks. A fossil lepidodendron, two fossil teeth, turtle bones, fossil coprolite, a fossil reptile jaw and other fossil remains have been found here.

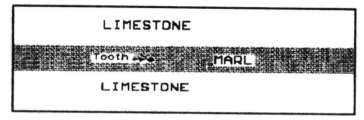

Figure 10 Tooth Location in Marl

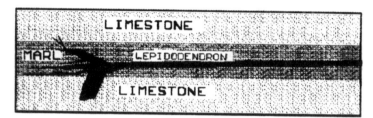

Figure 11 Lepidodendron Location in Marl

Cretacious limestone. It was compressed vertically but was approximately 42 inches wide at the base. Some of the root was embedded 8 inches into the second limestone layer with the main portion being in the clay marl and some extending into the upper limestone layer, thus making it a polystrate fossil. (A polystrate fossil is one that extends through two or more distinct sedimentary layers.) This demonstrates fast deposition of the layers involved. The clay marl layer is the same one in which the tooth was found, and with the lepidodendron about 6 feet from the tooth location.

For a diagram of the McFall II site where the tooth and lepidodendron were found, see Figure 8. Figure 9 shows the measured distances from the tooth location to the center toes of the dinosaur tracks that were used for reference. A sketch showing the vertical relationship of the tooth in the marl layer is shown in Figure 10, and the vertical relationship of the lepidodendron is shown in Figure 11.

The Creation Evidence Museum sponsored another dig activity from April 4-7, 1988. Two members of the Paluxy Task Force, Jerry Roth and Robert Helfinstine, participated in this activity. It began with additional

excavation of the lepidodendron. But since this fossil specimen extended in the direction of the adjacent county road, only a limited amount of it could be uncovered.

The rock directly adjacent to the tooth location was then removed, and excavation of the marl beneath this rock was done. Some extensions of the lepidodendron roots were found in the marl as well as a pycnodont (fossil fish) tooth. The pycnodont tooth was not an incisor type.

During the time we were at Glen Rose, we obtained some photographs of the fossil tooth found in 1987 compared with some pycnodont incisor teeth belonging to Ron Hastings. There are some similarities, but the differences are significant as will be shown in the analysis section of this report. We were informed that Dr. Petra Wilder-Smith, Dr. A. E. Wilder-Smith's daughter from Heidelberg, Germany, was in Texas the previous week investigating the tooth. After she had examined the tooth under a microscope and had reviewed SEM (scanning electron microscope) photos taken by Dr. David Menton she related that she had seen similar SEM photos of human teeth. However, to date none have been submitted for comparison.

Fossil Finger

We also obtained photos of a fossilized human finger found several miles from Glen Rose in SW Somervell County near Chalk Mountain. It was found by Mrs. Jessie Hitt on her property some years ago near where rock and gravel are quarried from deposits of Comanche Peak limestone near the Walnut Formation contact. The photos included X-rays of the fossil finger. We were shown the fossil finger and took additional photos of it. Figure 12 is an X-ray profile of the finger that matches the profile of modern fingers. A comparison photo showing the fossil finger with a live human finger is shown in Figure C-1.

The site where the finger was found was visited on April 7, 1988, primarily as a reconnaissance trip. No digging was allowed, but many fossils were visible in the loose limestone and in the crumbling limestone layers.

The hot, dry weather in the summer of 1988 caused the Paluxy River to recede to a low level, making ideal conditions for further investigation of tracks. Dr. John DeVilbiss and some associates excavated the Kerr site in an effort to extend a series of tracks leading up to an "island" in the river. This is located across the river from the McFall II ledge where Dr. Carl Baugh had been excavating. Based on indirect reports, nothing significant was found at this site. Additional excavation work was done at the McFall site where several dinosaur trails were extended.

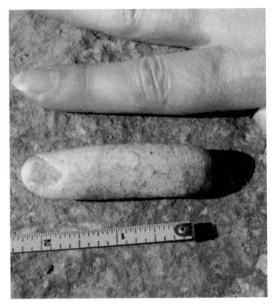

Figure C-1
Fossil finger by human finger for comparison

Trail Examination

Because of earlier finds of color prints without depressions, the low water conditions provided optimum viewing of this type of print. Ron Hastings, in a video recording made on Aug. 21, 1988, showed the clear color outlines of the Taylor trail, the Turnage trail, the giant run trail and portions of the 2DW, 2D and C trails. What he defined as the Ryals trail was not clear in the video because of the depth of water over the tracks. The so-called missing tracks in the giant run trail were shown by identifying color tracks without depressions. The video also showed how vivid the color prints become when water is put on the exposed dry limestone.

Hastings indicated that the Ryals trail is a series of dinosaur color prints in a part of the river that has been scoured by the main flow of the river. Additional investigation by Don Patton indicates that the true Ryals trail crosses the dinosaur trail at a 40-degree angle with a clear right human-like track superimposed across one of the dinosaur tracks. This track was used in the film *Footprints in Stone* to show the fit of a human

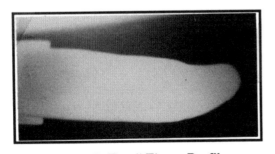

Figure 12 Fossil Finger Profile

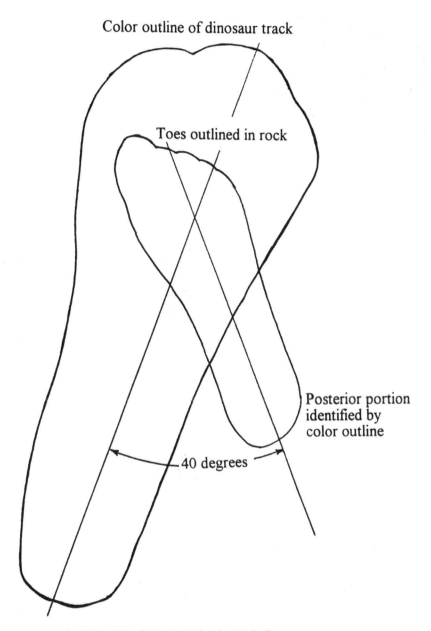

Color outline of dinosaur track

Toes outlined in rock

Posterior portion
identified by
color outline

40 degrees

Figure 13 Sketch of Ryals Print in Relation
to Dinosaur Track

Figure C-2
J. C. McFall by Taylor Trail, 1984. Print in foreground shows dinosaur track features.

Figure C-3
Portion of the Taylor Trail as seen in the mid 1970s showing tracks -3 to +3. The cross trail at print +1 is the IIDW dinosaur trail.

Figure C-5
Taylor Trail print +6, 1988, a left foot impression with mud push-up on the right side.

Figure C-4
Taylor Trail print -3B, 1988, a double right foot impression at the left side of an underlying dinosaur track that extends beyond the top of the photo.

Figure C-6
Taylor Trail print +6, 1992, showing position adjacent to 24-inch dinosaur track.

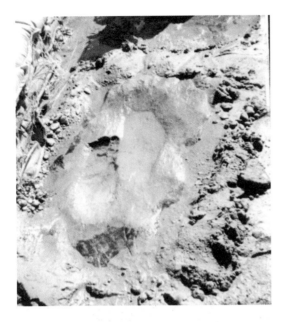

Figure C-7

An overhead view of Taylor Trail print +6 and dinosaur track, 1992, from 3D slide.

Figure C-8b

Enlargement of human-like track from C-7

Figure C-8a

Taylor Trail print +6, 1992, from overhead. Toe color outline has been enhanced by erosion. Arrow points to child track depression.

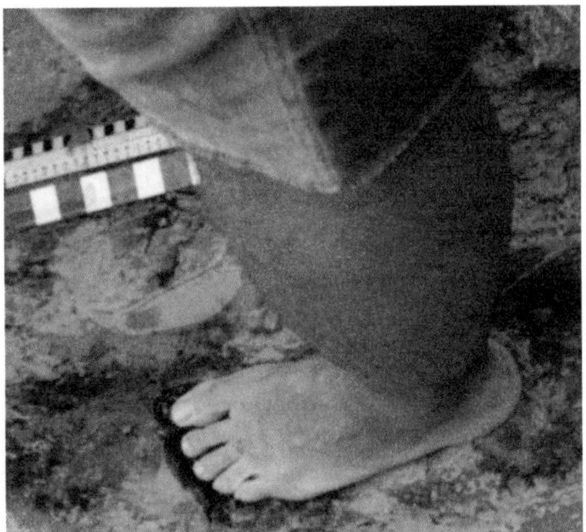

Figure C-9

Human foot in Taylor Trail print +6 depression. "A perfect fit"

Figure C-10
Professor Wilbur Fields by Clark print +3C,
a left print.

Figure C-11
Enlargement of Clark print +3C. Note mud
pull-up in big toe area.

Figure C-12
Clark left foot toe outline +1C with arrow showing direction of track.
Toe outline was adjacent to lepidodendron root.

foot in the fossil print. Immediately ahead, where a left print would be expected, is a hole left by Jim Ryals where he removed a track. Hastings indicated that the missing print in the Ryals trail is caused by removal of one of the dinosaur prints. However, there are references to Ryals removing a human-like track from near a dinosaur track. J. C. McFall, current owner of the McFall ranch, helped his father, Emmet McFall, and Jim Ryals move the piece of limestone with the footprint in Emmet McFall's truck. Figure 13 shows a diagram of the trail crossing area based on Patton's description. This can be compared with Figure C-37, a photograph of the superimposed track showing the toe depressions but with the heel portion defined by the color outline. Another view is shown in Figure C-38 with clear indication of toe drag marks on the surface above the toe depressions.

With the low water conditions, additional investigation of the Taylor trail was made

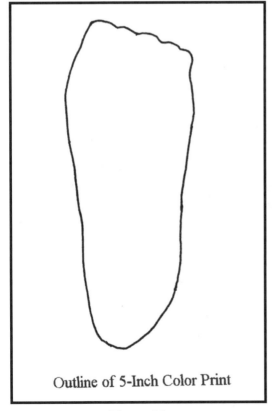

Outline of 5-Inch Color Print

Figure 14

by Patton and Baugh. There is no argument that the basic trail, as identified by the stain marks, are partially infilled tracks of a dinosaur. However, the depressions and mud pushup contours on some of the prints are not explained by the dinosaur tracks alone. Dual impressions have been identified in a number of the Taylor prints. One of the most impressive of these is shown in Figure C-4 from location -3B. Evidence of superimposed prints is also found in prints -2, +1, +3 and +5.

Additional color tracks, previously unidentified, were found in the search of the riverbed during the period of low water. One of these tracks is shown as an outline in Figure 14. It is 5 inches long and has the appearance of a child's footprint. Dr. Ron Hastings disagrees with this interpretation. He calls it a partial coloration of a small dinosaur track. (Hastings, R. J., 1989). It is located near the Taylor trail print +2. Because no distinct trail of this type of print has been found, it is only a reference for further investigation. A four-year-old child, after being shown a picture of a color dinosaur print, was shown the picture of this print without identifying what it was. She immediately called it a footprint and pointed to the toes. That was not a very scientific test, but it does show that it is not too difficult to discern the basic nature of the print.

Dr. John Morris visited the Paluxy river in September 1988 to see the evidence found during the low water period. His response to the newly acquired evidence was reported in the December 1988 *Acts and Facts* (Morris, John D., 1988) published by the Institute for Creation Research. Dr. Morris describes the secondary impressions inside the dinosaur tracks as "somewhat human-like impressions, each rather consistent in length." He observes that "The location and orientation of each is slightly different within each dinosaur track, and in several cases toe-like impressions are seen in the proper location

Figure C-13
Lepidodendron root section 9 ft. 8 inches long at McFall II site

and configuration." However, he concludes that "certain identification is lacking," and that objective data are needed. He then mentioned the tooth on which numerous tests have been conducted as an example of objective data gathering, which, if verified as being human, will presumably be a basis for saying that the tracks may also be of human origin.

This again brings up the question "what is needed for positive identification of human coexistence with dinosaurs and acceptance of the footprints thought to be of human origin?" Certainly, a human skeleton found in the Paluxy rock layers would be convincing. Based on one of our presuppositions that the limestone layers were laid down during the flood, and that humans were living at that time and likely left some of the prints in question, then there may be fossil human remains in the vicinity. But as stated earlier, only a small fraction of the possible resting place of such

evidence is available for investigation.

More Lepidodendron and Extension of the Clark Trail

Activity continued in April 1989 when a group from Tyler, Texas and others participated in a dig to examine a section of the McFall II site adjacent to the previous year's excavation. One of the objectives was to find the continuation of the Clark trail. Considerable time and effort in excavating the area had not been fruitless, but it had failed to reveal additional tracks leading up to the Clark print.

An additional track in the dinosaur trail going by the Clark print was found in the anticipated location. At right angles to it a second dinosaur

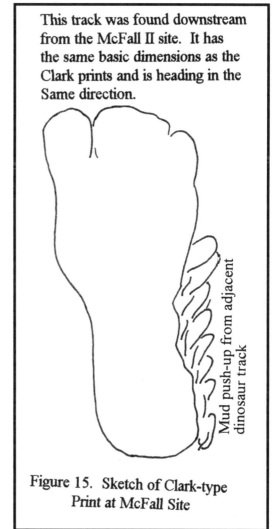

This track was found downstream from the McFall II site. It has the same basic dimensions as the Clark prints and is heading in the Same direction.

Mud push-up from adjacent dinosaur track

Figure 15. Sketch of Clark-type Print at McFall Site

trail of deep tracks was found, evidently made when the mud was very soft. The tracks were up to 7 inches deep. Because the group from Tyler, Texas contributed much of the effort in uncovering this trail, it was named the Tyler trail. Initial track identification was by letters A, B, C etc.

An extension of the lepidodendron root was also found in the area excavated. A length of 9 ft. 8 inches was uncovered in the marl layer and is shown as found in Figure C-13. Multiple-layered root terminations were found on a small side shoot from the larger root. A sketch of the area indicating the track locations relative to the lepidodendron is shown in Figure 8. Also found was a depression adjacent to the lepidodendron root which appears to be the anterior (front) of a human-like print of the same dimensions as that of the Clark print. Figure C-12 shows the toe outline. It is also a left footprint that coincides with the trail sequence. The individual making the track evidently put most of his foot on the lepidodendron root that was immediately adjacent to the toe track. The toe depressions are in the track way of the Clark print.

In August of 1989, during excavation work at the McFall site downstream from the McFall II site, the Hugh Miller team uncovered a man-like track adjacent to a dinosaur track but going in the opposite direction. The man-like track was made before the dinosaur track as evidenced by the mud flow from the dinosaur track pushing into the man-like track. It is a right footprint with fairly good toe details. It has the same dimensions as the Clark print farther upstream and is going in the same direction. Figure 15 is a sketch showing the general details of the track.

The variety of tracks and fossils found in this limited area makes it a site for continued excavation activity. A limiting factor in the southerly direction is the county road that covers most of the lepidodendron. However, there is still a considerable amount of the ledge between the road and the river to investigate.

Burdick Track

While at Glen Rose, a fossil human-like track that had been removed from rock strata at an unidentified location near the Paluxy River was examined. This distinct track, known as the Burdick track, has been in the Creation Evidence Museum for some years and has been the subject of some controversy. It is claimed by some to be a carving. Careful examination showed that the mud push-up between the first and second toes was distinctly higher than the rock surface around the print depression and that there is a mud push-up at the heel. Also, the smooth and dimpled surface of the track did not show signs of carving marks. On the contrary, in its natural state it appeared to be polished, a feature that a carver would find expensive considering all the irregularities in the print. The print had been sectioned through the ball of the foot to determine if pressure patterns were visible, but the results were inconclusive so the label of "carving" had been hanging on it.

In October 1989, it was decided by the staff of the Creation Evidence Museum to make a second lateral cut in the Burdick track, this time through the heel depression. Figure C-28 shows the track with the second cut in it. Definite pressure patterns were found. For comparison, several dinosaur tracks at the edge of the rock ledge along the riverbank were also sectioned without removing the track from the rock strata. Similar patterns were observed under some but not all track sections. Later, sections were cut through the toes of the Burdick track. These sections showed distinct pressure patterns. Details of the Burdick track are covered in the Analysis section.

The fossil finger was also sectioned to see if internal structure could be found by visual examination. Figure C-47 shows how the finger was sectioned. Definite details of skin,

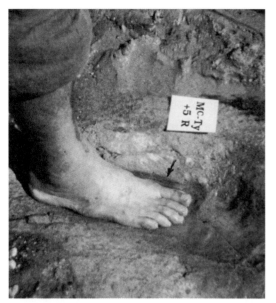

Figure C-14
Taylor Trail print +5, 1992, from 3D slide. Note lateral depression adjacent to bare foot. Arrow points to top of lateral depression.

---

flesh and bone were observed.

Burdick Track Site

In earlier discussions with Don Patton, the question was raised as to the possibility of finding the specific rock layer from which the Burdick track came. He had indicated that the probability of finding a specific rock layer would be small, and it would be hard to verify because of the general variation in the make-up of any given layer. After sectioning the Burdick track, it was determined that this rock layer was unique. A large number of crystalline calcite inclusions were embedded in this layer, some up to an inch or more in length. This rock layer is also very hard compared to some of the other layers, and not a likely candidate for carving. A search for the specific layer was aided by information that the track came from an overhang along the Cross Branch tributary of the Paluxy that joins the Paluxy in the city of Glen Rose.

In March 1991, the layer was located fairly high up the bank of Cross Branch Creek. Calcite inclusions were evident in the broken

ledge, a unique characteristic of the rock with the Burdick track. Those involved in the identification were John Watson of the Texas Water Commission, Dr. Carl Baugh of the Creation Evidence Museum, geologist Don Patton and Robert Helfinstine of the Paluxy Task Force.

New Evidence on Taylor Trail

During the week of August 17-22, 1992, the Taylor Trail was exposed for the first time since 1988. The previous week sand bags had been placed around much of the trail. Sand, mud and gravel had to be removed from the site before pumping out the water, and final cleanup of the tracks was required before documenting their condition. Several tracks had evidence of being damaged by a pointed object, particularly -3B and +1. It was of interest to note that when first uncovered the color outline of the dinosaur tracks was a bluish color, not red as was shown in the 1988 videos. The reddish surface layer of the limestone was now black in many areas. The infill areas were blue-gray, having been shielded from the light by the sand, mud and gravel.

Photographs taken of the Taylor trail in 1992 with a 3-D camera were not readily available for review at the time of publishing the first edition. Later, when looking at the 3-D slides, certain track features became very clear. Track +5, shown in Figure C-14, has a lateral depression on the left side of the right foot shown standing in the human-like track.

The revelations at the +6 track were spectacular. Details that were not apparent in the 1988 photo of this track (Figure C-5) are now clearly seen as human-like toe outlines in the 1992 photos of the same track shown in Figure C-6. The 1988 photo shows a distinct mud push-up. It had been suggested that the strong mud push-up surrounding and following the outline of this very human-like track indicated a dinosaur track, even though it was not as large as the other dinosaur impressions in this sequence. This suggestion is shown to be in error. In this sequence of tracks, those preceding +6 were shown to be human-like impressions superimposed on the dinosaur tracks. At the +6 location, erosion of the limestone surface revealed distinct red coloration of an obvious dinosaur track of 24-inch length conforming to the contour and dimensions of the dinosaur tracks in the rest of the trail. The startling fact was that the 11-inch very human-like track, surrounded by mud push-up, was completely outside of and beside this clear dinosaur track. Figure C-6 shows the relationship. Mud push-up does not surround erosion. This is a real, very human-like track in a series of 13 others of similar dimensions arranged in a left right pattern and side by side with a clear dinosaur track. The 1992 3-D photograph of the +6 track shown in Figure C-7, replaces the original Figure C-6. The overhead view presents a clear relationship between the dinosaur track, the 11-inch human-like track, and the small 5-inch child track.

Another Tooth

On the afternoon of August 18,1992 a small group went to the low water crossing downstream from the bridge by the museum to observe the dinosaur tracks in the exposed rock layers. There had been some indication that human-like tracks were also visible there. Although many dinosaur tracks were observed, nothing definitive was found that could be considered human-like. While examining the river bank, a number of fossil forms were identified in the crumbling limestone layers. A small pycnodont grinder tooth and a small reptilian tooth were found by Bob Helfinstine, both turned black by the chemicals in the rock. Will Zinke, who had been walking along with Bob, went on ahead while Bob was removing the pycnodont tooth from the rock. Will spotted a larger tooth, also black in color, a few feet farther along the ledge. It appeared to be a mammalian incisor with the labial surface (lip side) fully exposed. After being photographed in its

original location, see Figure C-41, a section of rock with the tooth was removed by Roger Fry. Gorman Gray also witnessed the tooth in its original location and its removal. It was taken to the Creation Evidence Museum for additional photographs and removal from the rock. Later, it was sent to Baylor Dental School in Dallas for analysis by Dr. James McIntosh. Details are given in the Analysis section.

More Tracks

Additional excavation work at the McFall II site began on August 19, 1992. The area had been cleared of debris the previous week. Three more dinosaur tracks from the Clark dinosaur trail were exposed, being numbered -1, -2 and -3 to be consistent with previous numbering. These were downstream from the Tyler trail of deep dinosaur tracks. The Tyler trail numbering was changed from A, B, C and D to 0, +1, +2 and +3. Adjacent to Clark dinosaur trail tracks -2 and –3, a two-foot section of a lepidodendron branch was excavated from the marl layer. It was identified by the circular patterns on its exterior surface.

Work continued at the McFall II site with several elongate depressions being uncovered. No specific pattern could be identified, either between the depressions or in relationship to the dinosaur trails. One depression by Clark dinosaur track number -3 appeared to have been made before the dinosaur track was made because of the mud displacement into the depression by the dinosaur track. One elongate depression near the rock ledge extended into a second depression going under the ledge. Upon further excavation, this second depression proved to be the +4 track of the Tyler trail of deep dinosaur tracks.

Figure C-15a – Hand Print

Figure C-15b – Hand Print with hand

LATE ADDITIONS

A Third Tooth

On Wednesday August 11, 1993 during excavation activities at the McFall II site, a third tooth was found in the same marl layer in which the first tooth was discovered. A young boy, breaking open pieces of the marl that was being removed, found the tooth and brought it to Dr. Baugh's attention. Its original location was approximately 21 feet downstream from that of the first tooth.

Although smaller than the first two teeth, it is within the size range of normal human teeth. The general morphology matches that of human teeth. See Figures C-43 and C-44 for labial and lingual views respectively. One dentist identified it as an upper right lateral incisor. The opinion of Dr. Ken Carlson of Minneapolis is that it could be a central incisor if it is a juvenile tooth.

On October 1, 1993 the tooth was taken to Dallas for analysis by Dr. James McIntosh at Baylor Dental School.

Mammalian Skull

This unique fossil specimen appears to be a partly compressed skull of a small mammal. The most prominent features of the fossil are the well-defined teeth on one side. Figure C-20 is a photo of that side.

The fossil is approximately 30 mm in length and appears to have been compressed before fossilization. Although it was not found in situ (in original location), it was found in Brazos River alluvium from an area that is predominantly Cretaceous deposits. It is made of redeposited calcium carbonate of the same color as the Cretaceous limestone in the area.

ADDITIONAL TRACKS

Since the publication of *Texas Tracks and Artifacts* in 1994, there has been additional track evidence found in Texas to support the recent-creation position that men and dinosaurs coexisted. The tracks further support the position that the limestone layers were first laid down as soft limestone mud which hardened soon after the tracks were made, and that subsequent layers were deposited soon afterward, thus preserving the tracks from erosion.

An Earlier Find

In 1934 Mr. A.M. Coffee of Stinnett, Texas, a pumper for the Gulf Oil Company, discovered a trail of nine "human-like footprints" in series on a rock ledge about four miles south of Stinnett. He worked one of the tracks loose and took it home. After he showed the artifact to a few friends, various interested persons removed the rest of the tracks from the site. The Coffee track is a right footprint measuring 8 ½ inches in length. On the rock slab adjacent to the Coffee footprint is a child's footprint. It is a left print about 5 inches long. The adult print is ¾ inches deep.

Clear toe imprints with mud pushup between the toes and slight mud displacement around the footprint provide a clear image of the foot that made the print. (Ref. Figure C–23)

The discovery of this series of tracks created an instant controversy among archaeologists, geologists and anthropologists, because the sedimentary rock system of the entire area is geologically assigned to the Permian (assumed to be 225 million years old). The general consensus was that the print had to be a carving made by Indians. The difficulties involved in drawing such conclusions were enhanced by the fact that the print was accompanied by eight other prints in the series, along with an adjacent child's print. Further controversy ensued when it was pointed out that the tracks were not "stylized" as other Indian carvings are.

Details of the track analysis are in Part II, Analysis of Information

Continuing Excavations

In July of 1996, a group of Japanese scientists, headed by a leading Japanese paleontologist Dr. Facuda, visited Glen Rose and the Paluxy River valley. Under the direction of Dr. Carl Baugh and with the participation of Joe Taylor, owner and director of Mount Blanco Fossil Museum of Crosbyton, Texas, they excavated a three-toed dinosaur track and an adjacent human-like track. Figure C-16 shows the track relationship. The Japanese became very excited with finding this combination of tracks, but since much of their conversation was in Japanese, the other participants didn't get the full benefit of what they were saying. The Japanese subsequently released a prime-time documentary in Japan verifying human tracks among the Paluxy dinosaur tracks.

In early 1997, a worker at a site in Palo Pinto County, Texas retrieved a Cretaceous limestone slab containing a human handprint. It is a left hand impression with the fingers spread in a manner indicating the person may have fallen. Figure C-15 - shown on page 43.

Figure C-16
Cast of Tracks Excavated by Japanese Scientists

The force of the fall was enough to push the thumb, index finger and middle finger an inch or more into the apparently thickening mud. The fall produced no splash marks in the mud. The distance from the tip of the thumb to the tip of the little finger is eight and one-half inches, the same spread as an average hand in a similar position. No additional excavation work has been done at this site. Geologist John Watson determined that the limestone at this location is the same formation that extends south into the Glen Rose area.

On July 3, 1997, during the scheduled excavation activity of the Creation Evidence Museum, a woman was cleaning out a large 3-toed dinosaur track on the McFall ledge that had been uncovered during the original excavations in April 1982. As she removed the hard clay at the bottom of the track, she noticed a secondary impression. It turned out to be a well-defined human-like track, the missing fourth track from a series of five. The human-like track is 9 1/2 inches long. Joe Taylor has made a replica of this track combination. A photograph of the track is shown in Figure C-17.

In the summer of 1999, the Paluxy River bed dried up because of hot, dry weather. Dr. Don Patton, geologist from Dallas, and Dr. Carl Baugh, of Creation Evidence Museum, examined the area of the Taylor Trail. They found several new tracks about 25 meters upstream from the Taylor Trail. Removal of additional limestone slabs revealed numerous dinosaur tracks. On one trail of dinosaur tracks there are 12 identified superimposed human-like tracks. This new trail of human-like tracks, superimposed on dinosaur tracks, is named the McFall trail. It ends where two "perfect human footprints" were cut out in the late 1940s by the late Emmit McFall and the Wilson brothers. A total of 175 new dinosaur tracks were documented. Figure mcf4 shows the +4 human-like print superimposed on a dinosaur print, one of a series of 10- inch, left/right impressions. Details include all 5 toes, instep and mud pushup around a depressed print. Figure C-22 is a view of the McFall trail.

Turnage-Patton Trail

The Texas drought of 2000 made new track discoveries possible. A platform in the Paluxy River bed near Glen Rose, Texas has been exposed by consulting geologist, Dr. Don Patton and volunteer workers, revealing three dramatic trails of dinosaur tracks. The primary trail consists of 136 consecutive tracks, extending over 400 feet. The prints are deep and incredibly detailed. The work of uncovering and cleaning the trails began September 9th and continued through October 14. It was conducted under the auspices of the Metroplex Institute Of Origin Science and the Creation Evidence Museum.

The primary trail is finally obscured at the upper end by erosion for a distance of about thirty feet and then the trail appears again for another twenty-one consecutive tracks, making a total of 157 tracks, extending over 500 feet. The upper section actually crosses the Taylor Trail. Another trail of twenty consecutive tracks has been uncovered beside the first at the lower end, going in the opposite direction. A third trail of twelve tracks has been found below the first two.

Field notes from investigations of the area in the late seventies indicate that Mike Turnage actually detected the long trail with his feet under several feet of water. In view of this, it has been determined that this exciting, historic new trail be designated "The Turnage-Patton Trail." Figure C-24.

The leading dinosaur track authorities have acknowledged that they know of no other single consecutive dinosaur trail in North America that is this long. Both the length and the beautifully preserved detail certainly make this one of the finest displays of dinosaur tracks in the world.

CEM Annual Excavation – 2003

Six new dinosaur footprints were excavated on the McFall ledge as well as one turtle bone and a 9¾-inch human-like left footprint designated a "Beverly" track. This shallow track has some mud push-up on the left side. Figure C-18 is an overhead view. Figure C-19 shows the foot of the landowner's daughter in the track. An unusual find during the excavation process was a worm fossil in a vertical position, a further indication of rapid sedimentation and lithification.

CEM Annual Excavation - 2004

No new human footprints were found, but the Acrocanthosaurus trackway was extended to 46 continuous footprints.

Tracks in other locations

The 9-inch Zapata track from New Mexico shows clear impressions of all 5 toes and well-defined arches. It was found in a remote area that abounds in fossil footprints of various animals as well as birds. The rock layer is classified as Permian by conventional geological dating. See Figure C-25

Figure C-17
Beverly track inside dinosaur
track on the McFall ledge, 1997

Figure C-19
Daughter of landowner with foot in
Beverly track

Figure C-18
Overhead view of Beverly track, 2003

Figure C-20
Fossil Jaw

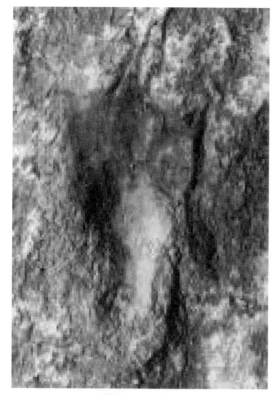

Figure C-21
McFall trail print +4 on dinosaur track

Figure C-22
View of the McFall trail

Figure C-23
Coffee Track from Stinnett, Texas

Figure C-24
The Turnage - Patton Trail

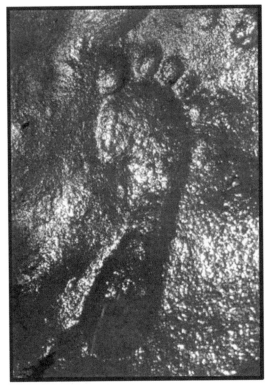

Figure C-25
Zapata Footprint from New Mexico

Figure C-26
Mother and Child Track from
Pennsylvania, natural color

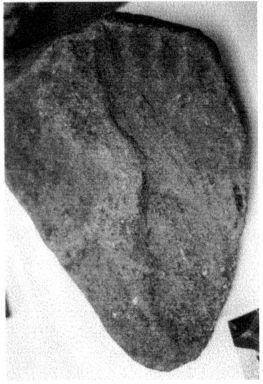

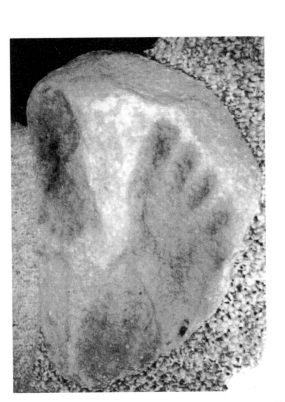

Figure C-27
Mother and Child Track in oblique light

48

The Kayenta formation near Tuba City, Arizona contains a variety of track impressions made by dinosaurs, mammals and apparent human-like creatures. Less distinct human-like tracks found in sequence along with more distinct individual tracks gives credibility to all of the prints. The details of the identification and mapping of these tracks are reported in the December 1989 Creation Research Quarterly. (Rosnau et al, 1989)

Dinosaur and human-like tracks have been found in the Dakota sandstone near Kenton, Oklahoma by Mr. Truman Tucker. Several types of mammal tracks have also been found there. (Beierle, Fredrick, p. 7, 8, 1980)

Jacobs' Mother and Child Print
The "Mother and Child" footprint rock was discovered by Paul Jacobs in 1995 on the bank of a small stream that had recently overflowed. The stream is located on Rattlesnake Mountain in Pennsylvania. The sandstone rock is classified as Mississippian, dated by conventional geology as being approximately 300 million years old. This right footprint is 9 inches long, has a well-defined arch and shows mud pushup on the edges and between the toes. The 6-inch child track, also a right footprint, is oriented with the toes pointing toward the heel of the mother.
Figure C-26 shows the track. Part of the right side of the heel has fractured away. And most of the little toe is missing, but the track is genuine and not a carving. A second view, Figure C-27, is photographed in oblique lighting. It shows more details of the child track and clarifies the little toe on the mother track.

Since the Mother and Child rock was found, additional small-child footprints have been found, some in left-right sequence. These small prints do not have distinct toe impressions, possibly because the weight of the individuals making the tracks was not enough to imprint the toes in the sand matrix that eventually turned to sandstone.

Reports of human and dinosaur tracks together came from the former Soviet Union country of Turkmenistan in 1983 by way of an English version of the Moscow News. (No. 24, p. 10) The Jurassic plateau where thousands of footprints are found is considered to be 200 million years old by conventional geology dating. The human-like prints were questioned by the Soviet press because of the philosophical position that men did not evolve until after dinosaurs had become extinct.
A later report in a 1 January 1995 edition of Komsomolskaya Pravda provided confirmation of the tracks, but the journalist, Alexander Bushev, passed off the human tracks as being from an extraterrestrial since the tracks were supposedly very old.

Recent examinations of the plateau have identified fossilized goat tracks surrounded by three-toed dinosaur tracks. In nearby Uzbekistan eighty-six consecutive horse tracks are located with dinosaur tracks in a "100 million"-year old rock stratum. Local scientists agreed that horses and dinosaurs lived together. (Swift, Dennis, Secrets of the Ica Stones and Nazca Lines, 2006, p. 136)

Human-like tracks found in volcanic ash near Puebla, Mexico have caused some controversy in the fields of archaeology and anthropology. Here again the philosophical positions of some scientific investigators cause them to reject the idea that the tracks could be from Homo sapiens. The ash layers have been dated at 40,000 years BP. Modern theory has established migration to North America at about 12,000 BP.
Although there are no dinosaur tracks reported in this location, human-like tracks are being found in various parts of the world in material related to documented catastrophic events.

Summary of Evidences

During the different periods of excavation activities, an ever-increasing number of tracks and fossils have been discovered and documented. These have been supplemented by fossils found in other locations.

Significant finds or events are:

Clark Trail of 5 tracks in sequence plus a similar track found farther downstream.

Three fossil teeth, readily identifiable as being of human morphology

A fossil lepidodendron, an out-of-place fossil according to standard geological dating.

A fossil finger of human morphology.

Definite overprinting on the Taylor Trail of human-like prints over dinosaur prints, and identification of side-by-side human-like and dinosaur tracks.
Clarification of Ryals track by color outline.

Authentication of the Burdick track by sectioning and finding pressure patterns.

Tyler Trail of deep dinosaur tracks crossing the Clark dinosaur trail.

Small mammal skull, an out-of-place fossil according to standard geological dating.

Bones from two dinosaurs have been excavated from the Cretaceous formations upstream from the McFall excavation sites. Details are in Dr. Carl Baugh's book Dinosaur. (Baugh, Carl E., 1987, Chapter Nine)

The Coffee Track, found near Stinnett, Texas in 1934, came to the attention of Creation Evidence Museum.

Japanese scientists excavated a human-like track adjacent to a dinosaur track.

A detailed human handprint was taken from Cretaceous limestone in Palo Pinto County in 1997.

The McFall Trail was discovered during a period of low water level.

The Turnage-Patton Trail was uncovered during low water conditions, producing the longest continuous dinosaur trail in North America.

M&C Track - Information on the Mother & Child Track, found in Pennsylvania in 1995, was provided.

Part II
ANALYSIS OF INFORMATION

This section reports the analysis of the significant finds in more explicit detail. The various types of information gathered during the investigation resulted in a variety of examinations. Some were very detailed and required considerable expert assistance. Subjects covered in the following pages include analysis of the Glen Rose limestone and the coloration stains, footprints, fossil teeth and the fossil finger. Information on the metal hammer found near London, Texas in the 1930s is included in Section III.

Analysis of the Rock

In April 1986, a sample of Glen Rose limestone from the ledge at the McFall site where Dr. Carl Baugh had been excavating for footprints was obtained for examination. The sample was basically gray limestone with an orange colored surface where minerals have penetrated the limestone. The purpose in examining the rock was to provide a basis of comparison with samples we hoped to obtain from the Taylor Trail that, at the time, was the primary area of investigation. While examining the rock sample, several unique features, which were not the primary purpose of the investigation, were identified and are included as part of this book.

This particular sample came from the second layer down, a layer that crumbles and flakes off when exposed to the weather. Characteristic of the limestone layers is the orange/red coloring at the surface that also extends into fractures in the rock. Figure 6, shown in the previous section, is a diagram of the rock coloration. The analysis was done at two locations on the sample, at the surface in the colored area and at a point internal to the layer where there was no coloring. The coloring had penetrated into the matrix approximately 0.05 to 0.15 inches in the particular sample that was analyzed. The rock surface is uneven. Between the upper colored layer and a second colored layer the marl layer varies from 0.5 to 1.25 inches. The total thickness of the rock layer from which the sample came varies from 7 to 10 inches in this particular area.

A Scanning Electron Microscope (SEM) with an Energy Dispersive Spectrometry (EDS) capability was used to identify the elements in the samples. Figure 16 shows the EDS spectrum printout of the results from the basic rock matrix, and Figure 17 shows the printout of the results from the colored layer. Silicon (Si) and calcium (Ca) were identified in the basic rock while the colored layer also indicated aluminum (Al), iron (Fe), titanium (Ti), potassium (K) and sulfur (S). It is probably the iron that produces the orange/red coloring. It would appear that the basic limestone did not contain iron, but after being laid down it was covered with mineral bearing water that deposited the iron, sulfur, aluminum, potassium and titanium in the limestone surface.

The identification of the elements in the Glen Rose limestone did not reveal anything unusual with the possible exception of sulfur found in the surface area. It is assumed that carbon and oxygen would also be present in the form of carbonates and silicates. They were not detected since the SEM was not operated in the mode for detecting these elements.

In addition to the mineral elements in the rock, clam shells, fossil clam casts, oyster shells and smaller hard shelled creatures are found in the limestone deposits along the Paluxy River. These can usually be seen with the naked eye. Fossil clam casts rather than half shells are an indication of sudden burial while the clams were still alive. Clam casts and portions of clam and oyster shells are also found in marl layers along the Paluxy River.

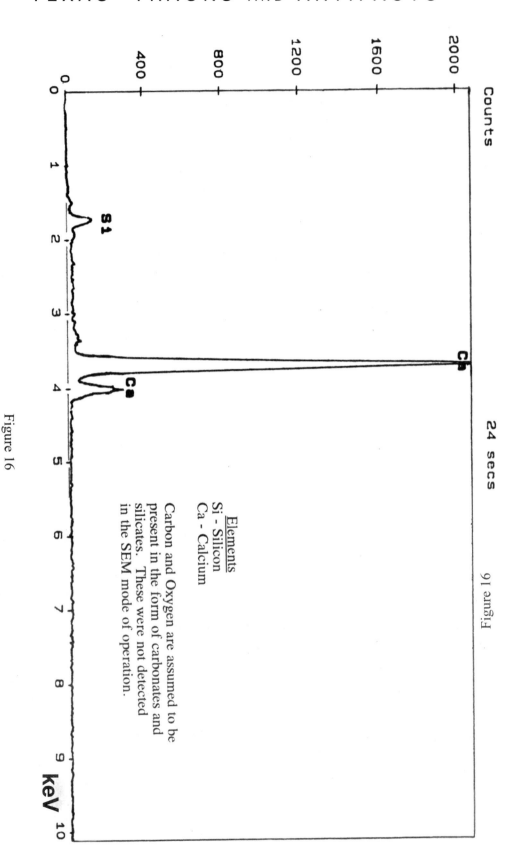

Figure 16

Identification of Elements in Glen Rose Limestone

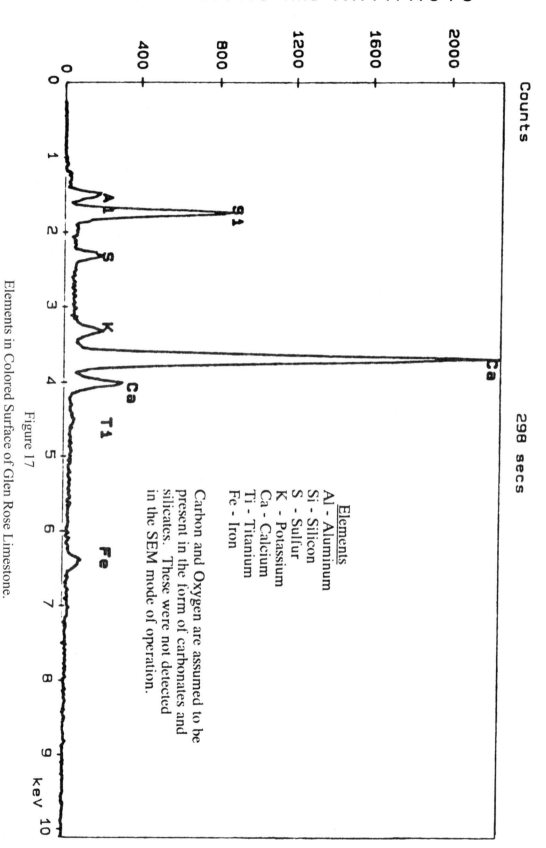

Figure 17

Elements in Colored Surface of Glen Rose Limestone.

Elements
Al - Aluminum
Si - Silicon
S - Sulfur
K - Potassium
Ca - Calcium
Ti - Titanium
Fe - Iron

Carbon and Oxygen are assumed to be present in the form of carbonates and silicates. These were not detected in the SEM mode of operation.

Several unusual specimens were found during the examination of the rock sample that was being used for chemical analysis of the rock. The first unusual life form found in the rock was a curved hair embedded in the rock matrix. When trying to reduce the rock fragment containing the hair to a sample small enough for SEM analysis, the sample was lost. A photograph using an optical microscope had been made, but the details were not magnified enough for identification.

The second unusual life form was first observed as a small dark spot in the rock sample. After some careful removal of adjacent rock material, a closer look at 60x magnification revealed this to be an insect whose legs were still embedded in the rock matrix. The insect was pliable, i.e., it was not a mineral replacement of the original material. Figure C-33 is a photo of the insect, and Figure C-34 is a photo of an enlarged section of one eye. The main portion of the insect was photographed using the SEM, and is shown in Figure 18. An attempt has been made to identify the insect, but as yet it has not been categorized.

Analysis of the Coloration Features

Figure 18 SEM Photo of Insect
(250X Magnification)
Insect was found by examining a spot in the Glen Rose limestone being analyzed for chemical composition.

Most of the Task Force's initial investigation into the true nature of the human-like prints, especially those of the Taylor Trail, centered on the determination of the coloration markings at the Taylor site. Since there were also dinosaur tracks that showed only as coloration outlines with only slight topographic relief, it was assumed that this feature might also be the key to understanding the Taylor Trail color patterns. This position was taken because it did not appear that the color features in question were man made as some had earlier suggested. Specific markings which were observed at the Taylor Trail in 1986 appeared "too neat" to be man made. It was also concluded that if someone wanted to make stain marks on the rock surface, coloring agents would not be needed since the rock layer already had a colored surface with a thin, light colored calcite over-layer. Removing the calcite in a specific pattern would temporarily show a "print" in the rock surface.

Reviewing photographs of the Taylor trail taken in 1984, clear dinosaur features are seen in several close-up pictures. Apparently those taking the pictures did not see these features until the renewed controversy caused a closer look. Figure C-1 is a reproduction of a 1984 photograph of J. C. McFall by the Taylor trail with the track +3 in the foreground, showing a partial dinosaur track outline and a smaller depression area within the track.

The nature of the coloration area was first indicated to the Paluxy Task Force in a letter from Dr. John Morris in June of 1986 in which he stated, "there is some evidence of toe infilling -although somewhat ambiguous". (Morris, John D., June 1986) This was based on his analysis of cores taken by John Mackay. Later in the year Dr. John Morris expressed some reservations about his tentative conclusions, but did indicate that there appeared to be no evidence of fraud. (Morris, John D., Sept. 1986)

While Dr. John Morris was analyzing the MacKay cores, Glen Kuban and Ron Hastings had also taken some cores for analysis. The Task force contacted Kuban in June 1986. Later in the year he sent us sketches of where the cores were taken on some specific tracks and photographs of several cores. The photographs show distinct lines between the stain area and the adjacent rock. Sample pictures and sketches are shown in Figures C-46 and 19. The indications are that the colored portion of the rock is infilled after the dinosaur walked through what was a fairly fresh layer of mud. According to Kuban, the blue-gray infilled portion is rich in iron which, when exposed to oxygen, moisture and sunlight and/or heat, changes color to a reddish brown due to oxidation of the iron. He also indicated that the material infilling the track is finer grained than that outside the track area. (Kuban, Glen J., 1986) Thin section and X-ray analysis of several core samples conducted by the Department of Earth and Space Sciences, Indiana/Purdue University at Fort Wayne, Indiana indicate that the infill material is largely dolomite with a small amount of calcite. The material around the infill has a majority of calcite and a small amount of dolomite. (Kuban, Glen J., 1986, p. 12). Sketches of Kuban's are the basis for the details shown in Figure 20 (Kuban, Glen J., 1986, p15), indicating the location of the cores and the nature of infilling from these particular samples. Kuban also reported that tracks, which were largely blue-gray appearance in 1984, had a red color in

1985. (Kuban, Glen J., 1986, p. 6). Exposure to sunlight seems to be a factor in the amount of red showing in the tracks. This was brought out clearly in August of 1992 when the Taylor trail was exposed. Figure C-6 shows the blue-

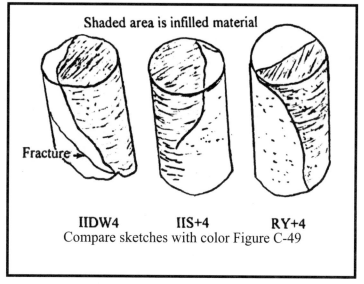

Shaded area is infilled material

Fracture →

IIDW4   IIS+4   RY+4
Compare sketches with color Figure C-49

Figure 19 Kuban core Details

gray color of the +6 Taylor track when the silt and gravel were first removed. After several days of sunshine, the blue-gray color could be seen in the background, but the surface color changed to a reddish brown as shown in Figure C-8b.

The exact process by which the tracks were infilled is unknown. There was evidently a period of time between when the original dinosaur track was made but before the print was covered by the marl layer that the finer grained material was washed into the track depression. Based on evidence obtained by visual examination and from core samples, it is certain that the coloration tracks are genuine. The identification of the Taylor trail as only human tracks was incomplete because the primary dinosaur track outlines were only partly visible at the time the trail was originally uncovered.

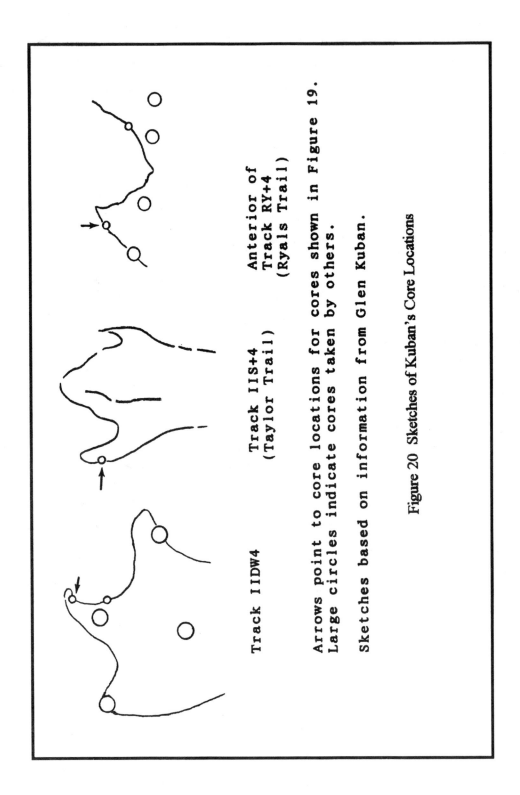

Track IIDW4

Track IIS+4
(Taylor Trail)

Anterior of
Track RY+4
(Ryals Trail)

Arrows point to core locations for cores shown in Figure 19.
Large circles indicate cores taken by others.

Sketches based on information from Glen Kuban.

Figure 20 Sketches of Kuban's Core Locations

Analysis of Footprints

The Taylor Trail, for a decade or so before the renewed controversy arose, had been used as evidence for the coexistence of dinosaurs and humans. But these were not the only human-like tracks found in this general area. As indicated earlier in this report, tracks found by Dr. Cecil Dougherty, Dr. John Morris, Dr. John DeVilbiss, Dr. Carl Baugh and others have provided a continuous but often brief display of evidence that appears to support the coexistence concept. It is the fragile nature of the tracks that has prevented more detailed analysis. That, along with restrictions on removing tracks for laboratory analysis, has slowed investigations considerably. Because of the renewed controversy on the Taylor Trail, the emphasis of the investigation was placed on finding other tracks and trails with good quality prints that could be used for evidence.

In the 25 or more years that Dr. Baugh has been excavating along the Paluxy, he has reported finding more than 90 human-like tracks and even more dinosaur tracks. A review of some of the reported human-like tracks in 1986 before they had completely eroded away showed that some were isolated depressions in the limestone surface and were not part of a distinct trail of left-right prints. They were similar in length and width to trail prints and were so identified even without the usual features of toes and arches.

Glen Kuban indicated that he and other co-workers had made measurements, had mapped and had photographed all the markings on the McFall ledge where Dr. Carl Baugh had been excavating. A pattern of isolated depressions with respect to a dinosaur trail was evident before the measurements were made. He concluded that the depressions might be tail marks because of their shape and position, or possibly toe or snout impressions. These could be made quite easily when the mud was soft. Explanations for isolated depressions do not explain others that appear in a definite sequence.

Observations of actual human tracks made in soft ground, mud of varying consistencies and in underwater mud show a wide variety of track forms. Variations in track formation depend on such things as:

1. Depth of mud
2. Texture of the material
3. Settling time of mud before track is made
4. Rate of foot insertion and withdrawal from mud
5. Direction of track maker, turning or straight-ahead

Tracks can show features such as elongated big toe, mud reflow over part of track and particularly the toes, mud push-up relating to depth of mud, mud consistency and rate of foot insertion, and cracks extending from toes in mud that has settled or is drying.

These variations in observed human tracks demonstrate the fact that individual tracks made under unknown conditions can be of a wide range of quality, in some cases making a positive identification difficult. Trail sequences where some of the tracks have enough clarity for identification can verify the less distinct tracks as being from the same track maker.

Analysis of specific tracks and trails follows:

Clark Trail
Quality of the prints identified as human has varied from questionable to poor to good. None found in recent years could be classified as excellent. The Clark print, uncovered in January 1987 and part of a trail that was investigated for several years, is a good print with clear evidence that the features identified are very human-like. The photograph shown

in Figure C-11 indicates the toes and general shape of a human footprint. This print is 14 inches long and approximately 5-1/4 inches wide at the ball of the foot. While some will argue that it is a print of some other animal, no one has identified what other creature has a footprint like a human being. Don Patton, while describing the Clark print at the 1992 Twin Cities Creation Conference, stated, "we had some from the Dallas Crime Lab forensic department examine this, and their conclusion was without doubt that this was a human track". (Patton, Don R., 1992)

Figure 8, referred to earlier, shows the Clark print (left) location relative to a dinosaur trail. The search for the next print in the reverse sequence had been frustrated since, in more than 10 feet of excavation in the general direction, no similar print has been found. From general observations, it was speculated that the next print (right) may have been obliterated by the dinosaur track a little over four feet back from the Clark print, and the previous left print may have been on a fossil lepidodendron which would have been a natural "stepping stone" for a person walking in mud. The fact that some of the heavy root of the lepidodendron was pushed into the limestone at first indicated that it could have been helped by the weight of the track-maker. However, this apparently was not the case, because in April 1989 a partial print was found by an extension of the lepidodendron root having the same basic toe dimensions as the Clark print. Careful examination of the dinosaur track, 4 feet back from the Clark track, revealed a curved contour the size and shape of a heel at the edge of the dinosaur print. Hope that the trail would yet be extended was given a big boost.

Figure C-12 shows the toe outline found by the lepidodendron root. Toe dimensions were the same as in the Clark print. The discontinuity between the 2nd and 3rd toes is not unusual for a person standing on something with the toes extended over the edge of the object.

For comparison, Figure 21 is the outline of a modern human footprint standing partly on the toes with part of the foot on a one inch object compared to the toe outline found by the lepidodendron root. The 4th and 5th toes tend to curl under since they do not put any pressure on the floor.

The total sequence of Clark prints now includes 5 covering a distance of just over 20 feet. The tracks have been numbered in reverse sequence from +5C to +1C with the detailed Clark print being +3C and the most recent toe outline being +1C. The +2C track is only shown by the heel outline next to a dinosaur track. Track spacing is fairly constant.

+5C to +4C, 60 inches heel to heel
+4C to +3C, 59 inches heel to heel
+3c to +2C, 60 inches heel to heel
+2C to +1C, 64 inches heel to toe,
(heel not visible)

Pushing off from the lepidodendron root and leaving only the toe mark in the mud may have aided the longer pace from +1C to +2C. It is evident that whoever made the tracks seemed to have been in a hurry since the pace is longer than the nominal walking pace of about 35 to 40 inches for a person having a 14-inch foot print. If in fact the dinosaur stepped on one of the human-like tracks, it is likely that the two track makers were in the area at the same time, and the approaching dinosaur may have provided some incentive for the track maker to move on.

A sequential profile of the Clark print was made from a cast of the print. Profiles are made with a contour gage. Figure C-36 shows a 12-inch contour gage on a cast of the Burdick track. Measurements on the Clark cast were made at half-inch intervals, and the contours were then drawn on paper and identified to preserve the profile. The individual profiles were then traced onto a scaled sheet of paper at the same intervals as they were measured.

Figure 22 shows the contour sequence. Toe details are not well defined with this profile spacing except for the big toe. This toe has a small mound in the middle of the depression evidently caused by the mud being pulled up as the foot was lifted up. This is consistent with the same kind of pull-up found in the adjacent dinosaur track about one foot away. Figure 24 shows the dinosaur track. The consistency of the mud at this particular spot was evidently just right to cause this pull-up characteristic. A second copy of Figure 22 with the approximate foot outline is shown as Figure 23 to aid in understanding the profile drawing.

For comparison with the Clark print, a sequential profile from a cast of the Caldwell print was made and is shown in Figure 25. We are using this 16-inch print only for comparison purposes. The Caldwell print is well known to many who have replicas of it. The original print was verified by geologist Billy Caldwell for whom the track was named. He had it removed from the limestone by the late Bill Osborne who also made a cast of the track for Caldwell. The original track was sold, and copies have been made from the cast. It has been called a carving by some because it is so well defined, but Caldwell insists that it is genuine (Baugh, Carl E., 1987, Page K in color section)) and taken from Cretaceous limestone along the Paluxy River near Glen Rose. There are many details in this track that an amateur carver would not include, and it is doubtful that a professional would spend his time on such a project. The Clark print is nearly as long as the Caldwell print, but it is narrower. Contours in the heel region are very similar. The Clark print is a left print, and the Caldwell print is a right print so this must be taken into consideration when making comparisons.

Detail examination of the Clark print and measurements of the contour were done by Mike Riddick of Arlington, Texas. The measurement data were sent to Professor

Clark left foot toe outline (+1C)

Arrows indicate direction of tracks.
Toe outline formed when
stepping over 1 inch object.

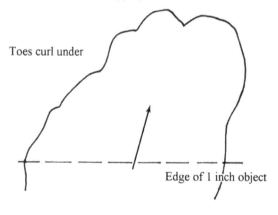

Figure 21 Actual Human Left Foot Toe Outline
Compared to Clark Track +1C Toe Outline

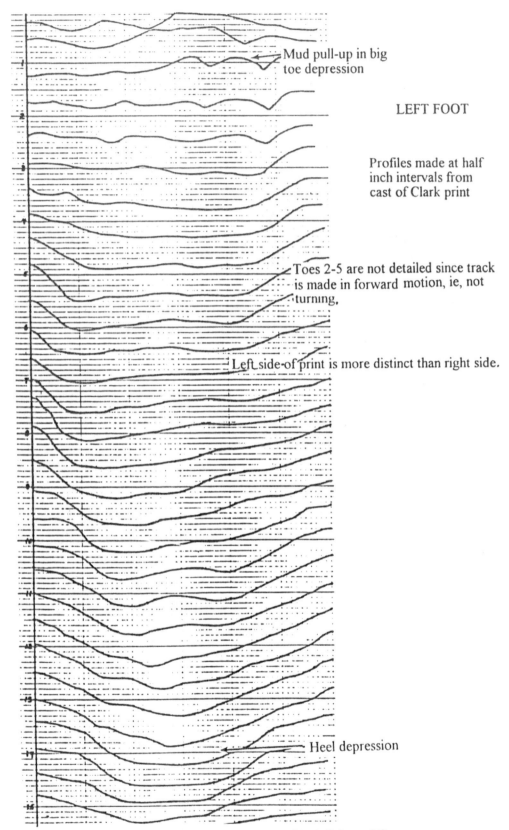

Mud pull-up in big toe depression

LEFT FOOT

Profiles made at half inch intervals from cast of Clark print

Toes 2-5 are not detailed since track is made in forward motion, ie, not turning.

Left side of print is more distinct than right side.

Heel depression

Figure 22 Profiles From Clark Print +3C

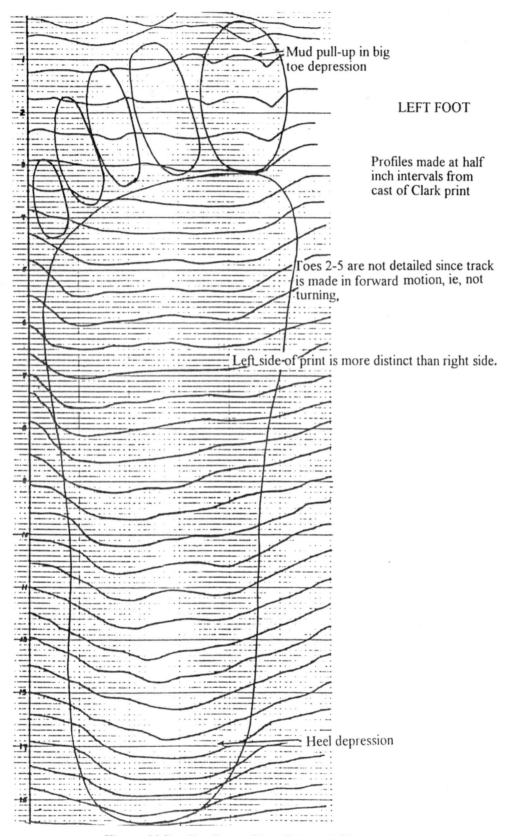

Mud pull-up in big
toe depression

LEFT FOOT

Profiles made at half
inch intervals from
cast of Clark print

Toes 2-5 are not detailed since track
is made in forward motion, ie, not
turning,

Left side of print is more distinct than right side.

Heel depression

Figure 23 Profiles From Clark Print +3C Modified

Figure 24 Dinosaur Track With Mud
Pull-up Located Adjacent to
Human-like Clark Print +3C

Marlyn Clark who, with the aid of a computer program, printed a contour profile of the track that is shown in Figure 26. Several toe details are evident in this figure, and can be compared to the photograph of the print shown in Figure C-11.

A contour drawing of the Laetoli print, found by Mary Leaky in Africa, is shown for comparison in Figure 27. This track has a much smoother profile since it was made in moist volcanic ash. It shows only details of the big toe, but the general area of the other toes is evident. There is no disagreement on the general shape of a human foot. The series of tracks found at Laetoli has been studied in detail by Russell Tuttle and reported in the March 1990 issue of Natural History. (Tuttle, Russell H., 1990) Tuttle's conclusions were that a "Lucy" type creature did not make the tracks, and primate tracks would not be mistaken for human tracks. Bear tracks, although similar, have detailed toe characteristics that distinguish them from human tracks since their big toe is on the outside of their foot. He stated, "If the G footprints were not known to be so old, we would readily conclude that they were made by a member of our genus, Homo." This is an example of philosophical beliefs overruling factual data.

By comparison, the Clark print contour details are not as smooth as those of the Laetoli print, and the nature of the medium in which the tracks were made has a lot to do with the difference. The limestone mud was not a homogeneous medium as indicated by examination of the rock. Harder inclusions and unequal hardening during the time the tracks were being made would minimize the chances of making an ideal track. Photos of the Clark print show a bump adjacent to the left side of the track that had some affect on the track. However, the general contour of the track from Figures 22 and 26 help in identifying it as a human-like footprint.

Study of tracks and toe details by Dr. Carl Baugh have produced information that indicates that most tracks produced by straight line walking do not give much toe details except for the big toe. However, when the person changes direction the toes push down on the foot on the outside of the turn. This can be easily verified by observing the difference in your own toe action while walking in a straight line compared to making a turn. Based on this information, it is not likely to find many tracks with detailed toe impressions.

Taylor Trail
In the late 1960's, in order to verify the coexistence of humans and dinosaurs and falsify the claim that all human-like tracks were carved, the Taylor team excavated under the Paluxy River bank by removing the overburden and a limestone layer. They originally exposed a trail of 9 tracks with left/right stride. The tracks were fresh, like they had just been made, and showing beautiful mud push-up around many of the tracks. Carving obviously can't be claimed for these tracks. As stated in the **Past History of Paluxy Track Finds** section of this book, original comments about the Taylor Trail were that the tracks appeared to be human-

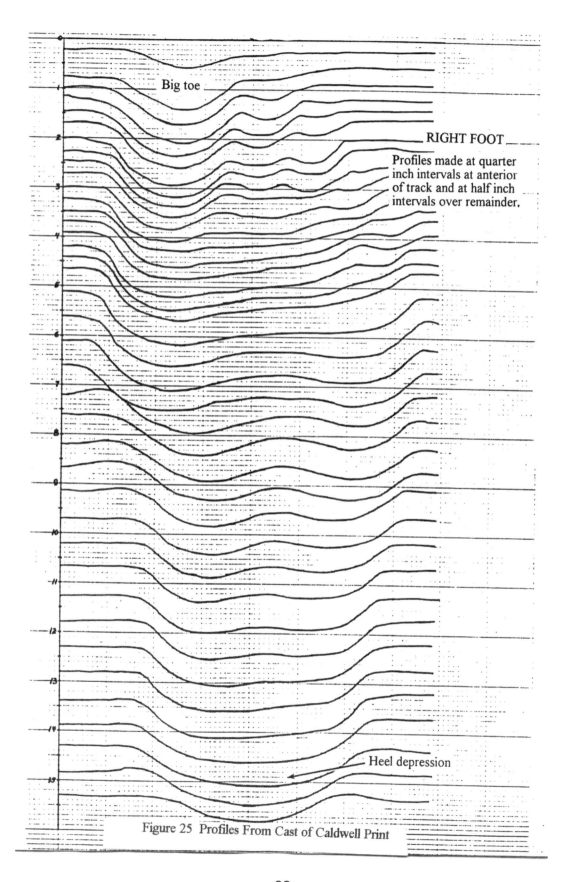

Big toe

RIGHT FOOT

Profiles made at quarter
inch intervals at anterior
of track and at half inch
intervals over remainder.

Heel depression

Figure 25 Profiles From Cast of Caldwell Print

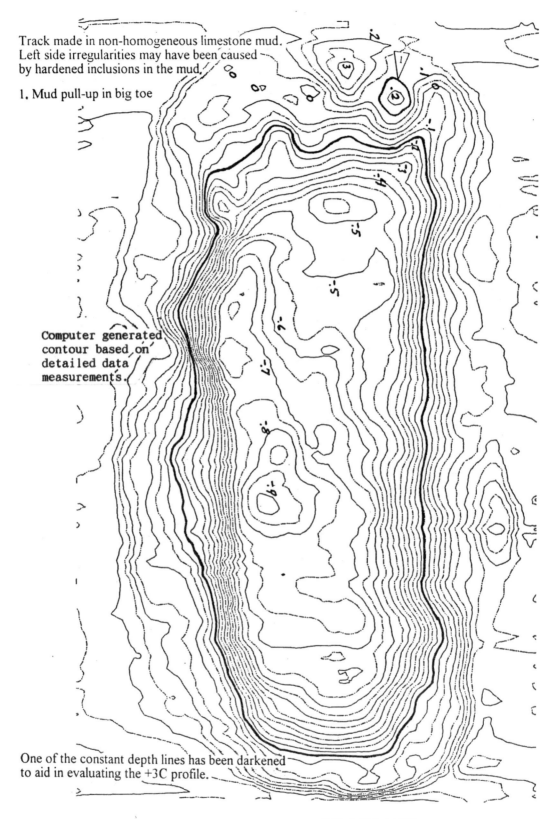

Track made in non-homogeneous limestone mud.
Left side irregularities may have been caused
by hardened inclusions in the mud.

1. Mud pull-up in big toe

Computer generated
contour based on
detailed data
measurements.

One of the constant depth lines has been darkened
to aid in evaluating the +3C profile.

Figure 26 Contour of Clark Print +3C

One of a series of tracks made in moist
volcanic ash. Laetoli, Tanzania, Africa

Note: Only big toe is defined
along with general out-
line of foot

Figure 27 Contour of Laetoli Print

like with clear detail of toes. A photo of the trail from the 1974-1978 time frame (Fig. C-3) shows considerably more mud push-up around the track depressions than was evident in 1986 when this investigation began. Early observers of the trail were evidently concentrating on what was found inside the mud push-up area. The comments by Dr. Block, Dr. Wright and Dr. Haddock, as reported in the earlier section on **Track Finders,** are significant when one considers that they saw the tracks before erosion had appreciably altered the details. They basically stated that the tracks looked like man tracks.

When we first started the task force activity we had all but written off the Taylor trail, but at least we wanted to see what it looked like. Looking only at the general depression area of a track gave little if any resemblance to a human track. Photographs of the trail available at that time provided some additional information and showed that the anterior was definitely dinosaurian. However, the size of the track depression appeared larger than the measurements given in Stan Taylor's notes.

Reviewing Dr. John Morris' pictures of the Taylor trail in the appendix of *Tracking Those Incredible Dinosaurs,* only overhead views were shown in which it was not easy to distinguish the track depression area. Morris did give a tabulation of track dimensions. Track lengths were mostly listed as 15 or 16 inches except for +3 and +4 at 18 inches and +6 as 11 inches. Width-at-toe dimensions were fairly consistent between 5 and 6 inches.

Taylor's note page (Figure 1), which identifies only 9 tracks, shows for track length four 9-inch tracks, one 11-inch track, three 12-inch tracks and one 16-inch track. Track widths are shown in a range from 2 to 4.5 inches at the "heel" area and from 2 to 8.5 inches in the anterior. The wide variation in Taylor's numbers is possibly an indication of mud slumping in some tracks.

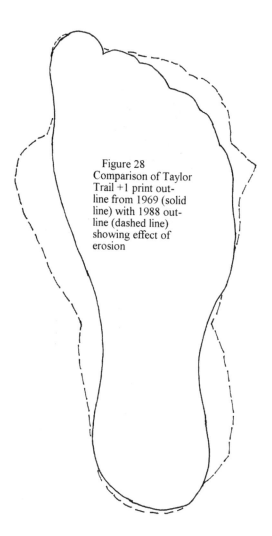

Figure 28
Comparison of Taylor Trail +1 print outline from 1969 (solid line) with 1988 outline (dashed line) showing effect of erosion

Comparing these two sets of numbers gives some indication of the amount of erosion that has taken place between Taylor's and Morris' measurements. Measuring techniques could also account for some differences.

As we see the trail now, erosion of the rock surface has removed much of the mud push-up that was evident in early photographs of the trail. It has also exposed additional color outlines of tridactyl dinosaur prints surrounding the eroded remains of human-like foot depressions.

Three things occurred after the dinosaur made his track. Initially there was some mud reflow, dominant in the anterior (toe) areas. The reflow was not consistent from track to track. Subsequent to this action, or possibly while it was still going on, the finer grained dolomite material began filling in the remaining dinosaur track depression. Whatever process provided the dolomite evidently ceased since it appears that the tracks were not completely filled. The dolomite material produced the coloration patterns when the trail was exposed. Curtailing of the dolomite flow is further substantiated by observation of the IID trail of dinosaur tracks. These deeper tracks were made after the Taylor trail tracks. IID track 7 depressed the mud push-up of Taylor track -4, with no evidence of dolomite infilling of the IID 7 track.

The discovery of the superimposed tracks in the Taylor trail by Patton and Baugh in 1988 opened a new series of investigations into these prints. Hastings continued insistence that these are only dinosaur tracks fails to account for the mud push-up or deep depression in the interior of the stain area that defines the general limits of the dinosaur track. While not all the superimposed tracks show toe details as does tracks -3B, there does appear to be a consistent left-right pattern in the trail, especially when you consider that variations are normal when walking in mud, and that erosion over the years has caused the loss of many of the original details.

Figure 28 is a comparison of the outline of the Taylor Trail +1 print from 1969 with a 1988 outline of the same print. The track has been widened in some places, showing the effects of erosion, but the general shape is still the same. The 1969 outline was based on a photograph of a cast of the print, and the 1988 outline was based on a direct photograph of the print.

Artist Jim Collins of Dallas made contour drawings of the Taylor tracks from a multiple photo analysis of 2D photographs. In reviewing these we find some details that we do not fully agree with when comparing them with photos and 3D slides. At least one, and maybe others, has been updated as new information has been made available.

The -3B contour drawing is shown in Figure 29 because this track has already been cited. The outline of the dinosaur track covers a larger area than that shown in Figure C-4 that includes the human-like superimposed track and a portion of the dinosaur track. This track was one of the clearest of the series showing significant detail of the human-like impression before it was defaced. It was actually a dual human-like impression. The shadow area at the top of the photo is evidently caused by the initial toe depression before the foot was fully settled in the dinosaur track. Extra toe marks are also indicated in the Figure 29 drawing of the -3B track.

At the 1992 Twin Cities Creation Conference, Don Patton showed how the human-type depressed area was located in different parts of the larger dinosaur print outline, and therefore evidence that the depression was not a characteristic of the dinosaur foot. Figure 30 shows several examples using tracks -3B, +1 and +4. These were chosen to show the variations in location. Track -3B secondary impression is located on the left central portion of the dinosaur track with the

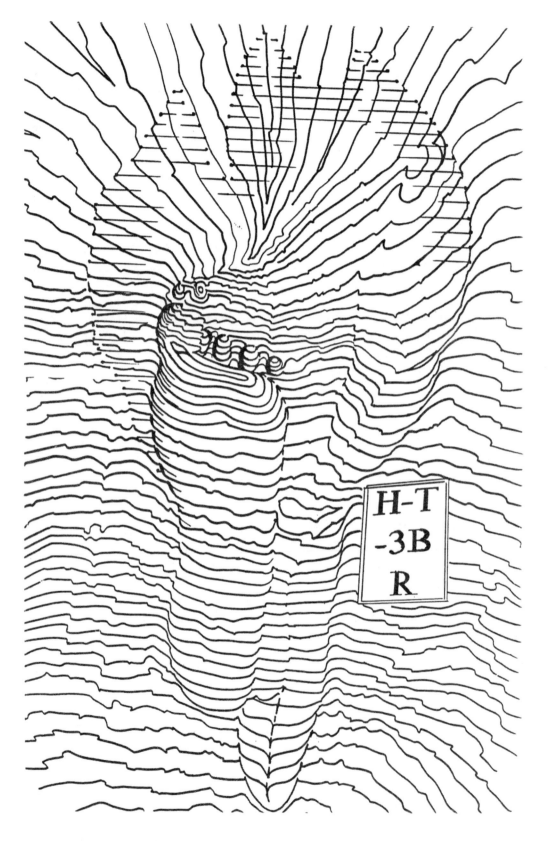

Figure 29 Artist Sketch of Taylor Track –3B

heel extending outside of the dinosaur track. Track +1 secondary impression is centered in the dinosaur track and slightly toward the posterior. The dinosaur anterior features are not clear in this track. Track +4 secondary impression is located in the right anterior portion of the dinosaur track. A summary of all Taylor track relationships is provided in Table 1.

If the mud was relatively soft at the time the secondary impressions were made, the track maker would find it easier to walk in already existing depressions than to struggle through the mud making his own tracks, even if he had to stretch his pace. The distance between tracks is not unreasonable. This has been demonstrated by putting a set of outlines on the ground in the pattern of the Taylor trail and having people walk on them. The walk was more of a loping gait, but 6-foot individuals had no problem adjusting their pace to the required distances. Also, one intentionally following the dinosaur trail would not be trying to place his foot in the same part of the dinosaur depression. There would be variations as has been shown. It is a similar situation to walking through 12 inches of semi-compacted wet snow. Based on personal experience, making new tracks is tiring, but following existing tracks, even with a different pace, is considerably easier. And you don't always hit the center of the existing track, resulting in some extra sliding of the feet.

Overprinting, as identified by R. Tuttle from his study of tracks and human track making, is a fairly normal characteristic. He also concluded that walking bare foot seemed to strengthen the arch and caused a separation between the big toe and the others. (Tuttle, Russell H., 1990) The human-like overprinting characteristics in the Taylor Trail have a consistent length of about 11 1/2 inches, they follow a consistent left-right sequence, and they are not in the same location in the dinosaur prints.

Re-examination of a portion of the Taylor Trail after the *1992 Twin Cities Creation Conference* showed that additional erosion had occurred since the 1988 exposure of the trail. One result of the erosion was to expose further details of the +6 print. The original size of this print, about 11 inches in length, did not fit the longer 24-inch coloration print size of the dinosaur tracks leading up to this location or the elongated depression areas averaging about 16 inches. The difference was shown in Glen Kuban's mapping of the Taylor Site. His drawing of the +6 track was much smaller than the drawing of tracks leading up to it. However, the 11-inch +6 print is consistent in size with the human-like tracks within the dinosaur tracks, but here the tracks are not superimposed but side-by-side. Erosion has revealed a 24-inch dinosaur print beside the clear 11-inch human-like print as shown in Figures C-6 and C-7. The two superimposed trails have now separated, and the details are clearly defined by impressions and color outlines. A section of Kuban's map from the Spring/Summer 1986 issue of *Origins Research* is shown as Figure 31 with an arrow pointing to the added dinosaur track beside what we interpret as the +6 human-like track.

The fit of the +6 track to a human foot is evident by comparing Figure C-8a, an overhead photo of the track as it appeared when first uncovered in 1992, with Figure C-9. Roger Fry, whose foot is shown in the track, stated that it was a perfect fit.

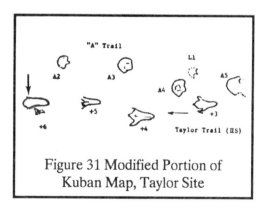

Figure 31 Modified Portion of Kuban Map, Taylor Site

Table 1
Taylor Trail Secondary Human-like Impressions

Track Number	Relation to Dinosaur Track	Track Number	Relation to Dinosaur Track
-7	Posterior*- Left	-1	Central - Toward Posterior
-6	Posterior - Central	+1	Central
-5	Central	+2	Upper Central - Toward Left
-4	Central - Slightly Left	+3	Posterior - Central
-3C	Central	+4	Anterior - Right
-3B	Central - Left	+5	Upper Central - Toward Left
-3	Anterior - Central	+6	Outside of Dinosaur Track - Left
-2	Central		

* Posterior = back, Anterior = front

This information is obtained from photographs of the Taylor Trail tracks which have been on public display a number of times including the 1992 Twin Cities Creation Conference and the 1993 Science Fair at the Creation Evidence Museum.

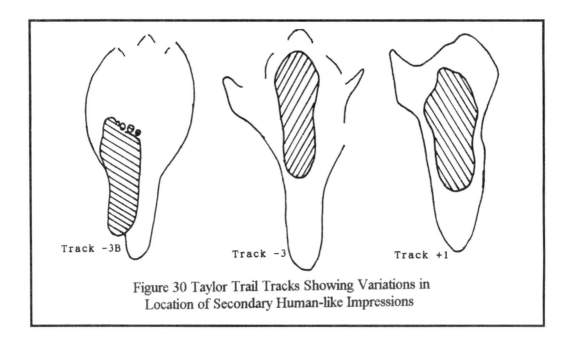

Figure 30 Taylor Trail Tracks Showing Variations in Location of Secondary Human-like Impressions

What was discovered later when studying 3D views of this track was that the notch in the mud push-up on the right central side of the print contour was a toe mark from another 5-inch track. This secondary track is angled about 30 degrees CW relative to the +6 track.

Figure C-14 is a print of the +5 Taylor track made from a 3-D slide. The lateral depression at the bottom of the dinosaur track matches the contour of a right human foot as shown in the picture. If the person stepping into the dinosaur track depression had slipped to the left, the contact with the soft mud would be recorded as depression shown.

At the *1992 Twin Cities Creation Conference*, Dr. Paul Ackerman related the details of a double blind test of "track identification" conducted at Wichita State University. Full-scale photographs of the 14 Taylor Trail prints were randomly numbered in various orientations and without any size scale indicated on them. They were shown to 8 students with the first question, "What are they?" Four of the 8 said they were footprints.

After indicating that the photos were scaled to normal size, the students were asked if there was any recognizable shape. Five of the 8 stated that they were footprint forms.

On the third step of the procedure the photos were identified as being of human footprint form, and the students were asked to arrange them in the toes-up position. Thirteen of the 14 were placed in the correct position with one being listed as ambiguous.

In the fourth test, the photos were arranged in the correct toe-up position. The students were then asked to identify each print as either a "left" or "right" track. Nine of the 14 were correctly identified, two were misidentified and 3 were undefined. These numbers agree with the general conclusions by those who photographed them. The left or right orientation was known only by their relative position in the trail for some of the prints.

Comments by the students as to the authenticity of the prints were that 4 stated that they were definitely footprints, 3 stated that they probably were footprints and one stated that they were probably not footprints.

These students had no special interest in these tracks. The results of the test indicate that there is information in the prints even though there has been considerable erosion of some features.

We recognize that the quality of these prints are less than desirable to make an airtight case to satisfy critics who want toe and heel details on every track. But careful examination of details in the data that we have shows a consistency in dimensions and left-right pattern.

Becky Print

The small 5-inch track outline shown in Figure 14 has been compared with several foot outlines from modern children ranging in age from 22 months to 4 years. Figure 32 shows the modern outlines compared to the fossil outline. Identification is as follows:

A. 22-monthboy
   5 1/2 X 2 3/8 inches
B 2 ½-year old girl
   5 1/2 X 2 1/2 inches
C. 3-year old girl
   5 3/4 X 2 1/2 inches
D. fossil outline
   5 X 2 1/4   inches
E. 2-year old girl
   5 1/2 X 2 1/8 inches
F. 3-year old boy
   6 X 2 3/8   inches
G. 4-year old girl
   6 1/4 X 2 3/4 inches

H. 3-year old boy
   6 X 2 1/2 inches
J. 4-year old boy
   6 1/4 X 2 1/2 inches

The modern outlines were obtained from children who are Caucasian except for the 4 year old girl, G, who is oriental. No two were from the same biological parents. The range of ages shows that the main variation is in length with the width being fairly constant. The fossil print is slightly smaller than the comparison samples, but the length to width ratio is approximately the same. The difference in size may be due in part to the way the children's outlines were obtained. Outlines were made to equal the total width of the foot. An actual footprint would be somewhat smaller, depending on the nature of the material on which it was made.

The closest match in length and width is between D, the fossil outline, and E, the 2-year old girl, but there is a distinct difference in the slope of the toe line. The closest match in the slope of the toe line is between D and H. Foot outline variations among the samples show that no fixed pattern exists. There is a high probability of this fossil outline being a genuine track since several others have been found in the same area, although none in sequence.

The 5 track locations are:

   1. Adjacent to Taylor track +1
   2. In Taylor track +4
   3. In Taylor track -6
   4. In Taylor track +6
   5. In the Ryals track.

Mother and Child Track

Some of the information relating to this pair of tracks referred to the child as a baby. However, the six-inch foot length seems to indicate a slightly older child. The eight children's tracks that were compared to the Becky track

in Figure 32 ranged in length from 5½ to 6¼ inches with the longer tracks belonging to 3 and 4 year olds. On a comparison basis, the age of the child represented in the Mother and Child track would appear to be in the 3 to 4 year old range. The nine-inch mother track appears normal for a woman from 60 to 66 inches in height.

Burdick Track

The Burdick track has good toe details as would be expected if the individual making the track were turning left or possibly running. As mentioned earlier, this track has been called a carving because it is such a good print. To test the carving theory, the track was sectioned in several places. Figure C-28 shows the Burdick track with the first two of the sectioning lines clearly identified. The section through the ball of the foot had not shown any significant details; particularly there were no laminations. Because there are no laminations, different pressure indications have to be identified.

The section through the heel (Figure C-29) shows that the limestone directly beneath the heel depression has a different pattern than the remainder of the stone. Small swirls and circular patterns are evident indicating a disturbance to that part of the rock matrix before it hardened. This compares with similar patterns found by Baugh and Patton in the sections of some dinosaur tracks. Several other things are evident in this photo. First, the crystalline calcite inclusion under the heel depression is an identifying characteristic of the rock layer from which the track came. Second, the non-homogeneous nature of the rock matrix is shown by the various color changes. Third, the arch profile is clearly shown at the top of the photo.

The third and fourth sections made through the toes showed the most distinctive disturbance patterns. Figure C-30 is a black-light photo from a section through the toes. Details are enhanced with this type of photography.

No two children from same biological parents.
All Caucasian except girl G, an Oriental.

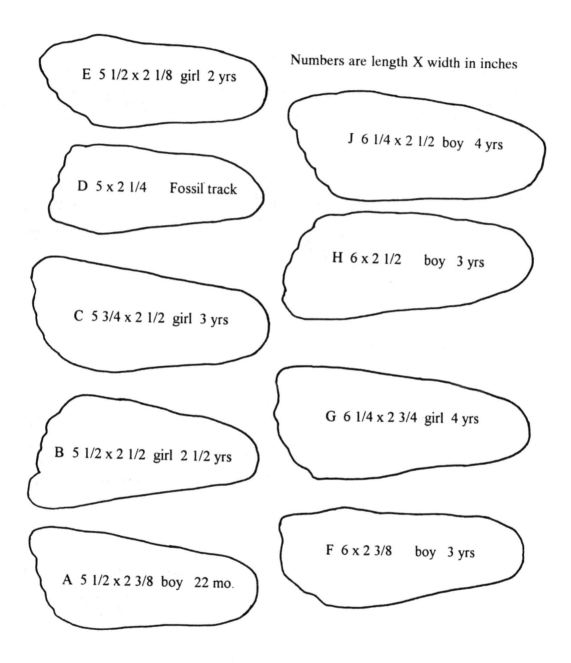

Numbers are length X width in inches

E 5 1/2 x 2 1/8 girl 2 yrs

J 6 1/4 x 2 1/2 boy 4 yrs

D 5 x 2 1/4   Fossil track

H 6 x 2 1/2   boy 3 yrs

C 5 3/4 x 2 1/2 girl 3 yrs

G 6 1/4 x 2 3/4 girl 4 yrs

B 5 1/2 x 2 1/2 girl 2 1/2 yrs

A 5 1/2 x 2 3/8 boy 22 mo.

F 6 x 2 3/8   boy 3 yrs

Figure 32 Comparison of Children's Foot
Outlines With Fossil Track Outline

Figure C-28
Burdick track showing the first two sectioning cuts.

Figure C-29
Burdick track section through the heel. Disturbed area is above the white calcite crystal inclusion. Note arch contour on upper surface.

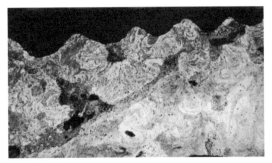

Figure C-30
Black light photo of Burdick track section through toes. Big toe on left. Note pressure structure under inclusion beneath second toe.

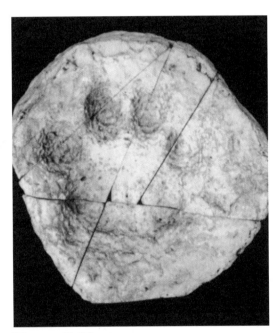

Figure C-31
Cat track, 9 inches in diameter, showing sectioning.

Figure C-32
Cat track section showing depressed laminations.

Some of the markings are apparently from small algal structures. But some features follow the toe contours, and in areas below the toes, pressure patterns are evident as indicated by the "moustache" shape below the inclusion under the second toe.

An earlier track that was sectioned and showed laminations under the print was a large cat track reportedly found in Glen Rose limestone. At the time it was sectioned it belonged to Clifford Burdick (Morris, John D., 1980, p.122). Figure 33 is from an old photo showing both the Burdick track and the cat track before they were sectioned. Since the Burdick man-track is 15 inches long, the cat track is approximately 9 inches from top to bottom. Sectioning of the cat track is shown in Figure C-31. Figure C-32 is a black light photo of one cat track section showing the lamination line that is evidence that the track is genuine.

The width to length ratio of the Burdick track has been cited as being too large in comparison with modern human prints. Tuttle's statement in the Natural History article indicates that barefoot people develop wider feet, and to support that statement he shows his foot in comparison to an Indian foot. The Indian foot has the same shape and width to length ratio as the Burdick track. From the *Journal of Forensic Sciences*, March 1988, under Barefoot Impressions are data showing a wide variety of adult footprint patterns (Laskowski and Kyle, 1988). The Burdick track fits within the charts that document the normal range of size, width to length ratios and other features.

As mentioned earlier, the rock ledge from which the track came was located along Cross Branch Creek in Glen Rose, being identified by the crystalline calcite inclusions in the rock. A further verification was made by a thin section comparison that was a perfect match.

A profile sequence of the Burdick track is shown in Figure 34 for comparison with the other print profiles. A modified profile showing the general foot outline is shown in Figure 35.

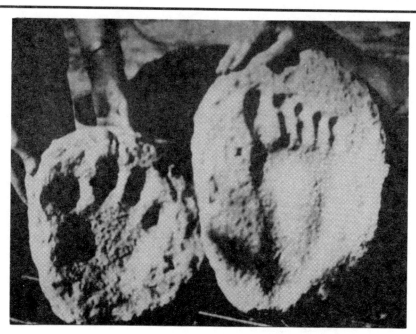

Figure 33 Cat Track With Burdick Track

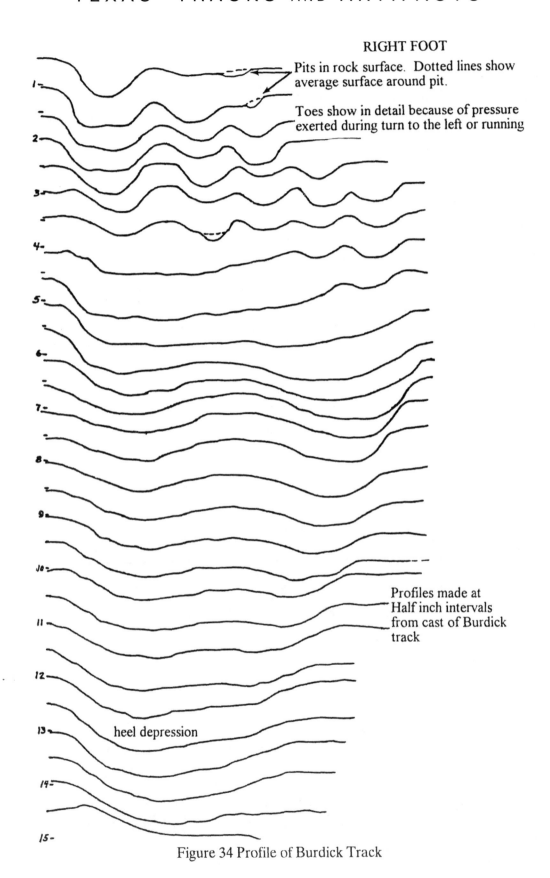

RIGHT FOOT

Pits in rock surface. Dotted lines show average surface around pit.

Toes show in detail because of pressure exerted during turn to the left or running

Profiles made at Half inch intervals from cast of Burdick track

heel depression

Figure 34 Profile of Burdick Track

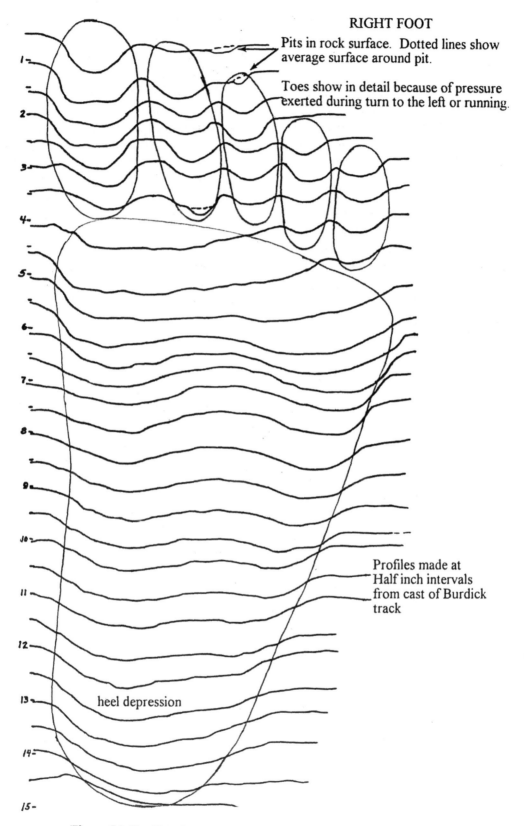

RIGHT FOOT

Pits in rock surface. Dotted lines show average surface around pit.

Toes show in detail because of pressure exerted during turn to the left or running.

Profiles made at Half inch intervals from cast of Burdick track

heel depression

Figure 35 Profile of Burdick Track Modified

Comparison of the Burdick and Australian track characteristics

There are numerous individuals who have examined the Burdick track or have studied the detailed information about the track that still insist that it is a carving. Since it was not found as part of a trail, there had been no other tracks to use for comparison until recently.

A number of human fossil tracks from Australia have been brought to our attention. They come from the Willandra Lakes district of western New South Wales, part of Mungo National Park. An aboriginal woman made the discovery in 2003 during an archaeology survey of the area. Erosion had uncovered what once was a muddy plain exposing 89 human footprints. An initial excavation uncovered 35 more tracks, and continuing excavations have revealed nearly 500 footprints, a mixture of children and adult tracks. (Webb, S., Cupper, M. L., Robins, R., 2006). Track lengths vary from 13 to 30 centimeters. 30 centimeters is 11.8 inches, which is not an excessively long foot. Skeletal remains, which had been uncovered in the vicinity several years earlier, had heights of 6 ft 4 in and 6 ft 6 in.

Of the prints left by six large adults, two sets were comparable to the Burdick track. Figures C-33 and C-34 show two of these tracks. The ruler in one picture is a 20-centimeter metric ruler. If the adjacent track is 30 cm (11.8 inches) long, it is shorter than the Burdick track, but useful for making a comparison because both are barefoot impressions made in similar calcium carbonate mud that hardened to preserve the tracks. The Figure C-34 track appears more like the Burdick track. A third track is shown in Figure 36. It is apparently from the same track way as the number 1 track since it is 30 centimeters long as evidenced by the 20-centimeter scale beside it.

The Australia tracks are in post-flood sediments. They are declared to be human tracks by Matthew L. Cupper of the University of Melbourne. (Webb, Cupper and Robins, 2006) They attribute the track makers to be Stone Age individuals from about 20,000 years ago based on optically stimulated luminescence (OSL) dating (Hunley et al, 1985; Aitken, 1998) of the burial ages of quartz sand grains from sediments above and below the track layer. .

Footprint measurement characteristics have previously been established and documented. (Garbe, Miller, et al,1992, pp 7-13.) Table X from their report, summarizes the human characteristics of the fossil footprints with those standards obtained from two separate sources in anthropological studies. As can be seen by comparing the measured results, there is no difference between the modern and the fossil foot parameters. At the time the report was written, nearly 50 human-like ichnites had been reported at the McFall site by the Paluxy River near Glen Rose, Texas. The writers of the report studied eight of the tracks that they helped to expose in the Cretaceous strata.

Using casts of the Burdick, Caldwell, Clark and Zapata tracks, and photographs of the three Australian tracks, measurements were made and aspect ratios were calculated. Measurements scaled from photographs are approximated in areas of shadow or indefinite boundaries. Results are presented in Table 2 Several tracks have parameters outside the ranges indicated in Table X. The conditions under which the tracks were made, including running on an unstable surface, would tend to produce variable parameters. Figure C-35 shows a section of track ways on the hardened mud flats where the three footprints used in the comparison were photographed. Notice the variations in the foot profiles in a given track way.

Sampling track dimensions from Table 1 of

Table 2 Aspect Ratio Characteristics *

	R-1	R-2	R-3	Taper
Caldwell track (cast)	2.4	1.5	2	39 deg.
Clark Track (cast)	2.8	1.5	2	35 deg.
Burdick track (cast)	2.1	1.7	2	25 deg.
Zapata track ** (cast)	2.6	1.5	1.9	36 deg.
Aus 1 (photo)	2.4	1.8	2	30 deg.
Aus 2 (photo)	2.2	1.5	2	32 deg.
Aus 3 (photo)	3.0	1.1	2	34 deg.

* R-1 = Foot length divided by ball width
R-2 = Ball width divided by heel width
R-3 = Width of great toe divided by average width of other toes.

** The Zapata track is very shallow, so some approximations were made for actual length and width measurements.

the Webb, Cupper, Robins report, the R-1 ratios varied from 2.3 to 3.3. Some of the variation can be attributed to the fact that the short children's tracks had higher ratios. Also, some of the tracks were from running trails. Table 2 of their report listed 8 trails of multiple tracks. Using the formula [velocity = stride length x 1.670 – 0.645] km/hr. (Cavanagh and Kram, 1989), the calculated velocities were from 5 to 20 km/hr.

All of this information indicates that the variations in individual foot print parameters represents natural physical variability in a diverse group of humans who all were barefoot.

The only apparent reason for evolutionists, or some long age creationists, not calling the Burdick track a human track is because of the Cretaceous rock layer it came from. But creationists who still insist that it is a carving have only their own personal biases for support.

Ryals Trail

Recognition of coloration features that help to define tracks in the limestone of the riverbed has also aided in defining the true nature of the Ryals track shown in Figure C-37. The anterior of the dinosaur track, which is only partially shown by coloration outlines, is not seen in older photographs of this track dating back to the mid 1970s. Nor did the older photographs show the posterior portion of the human-like track as a coloration outline as is now evident in Figure C-37.

TABLE X (From Garbe, Miller et al, 1992)
COMPARISON OF ASPECT CHARACTERISTICS OF FOSSIL HUMAN-
LIKE ICHNITES WITH THOSE OF THE MODERN HUMAN FOOT.

Aspect Ratio Characteristics	Aspect ratio averages/ (range)	
	Modern (a)	Ichnites (b)
R-1 (c)	2.5 (2.19 - 2.84)	2.6 (2.2 - 2.8)
R-2 (c)	1.47 (1.35 – 1.86)	1.45 (1.2 – 1.58)
R-3 (c)	2.0	2.0
Toe taper angle (Approximate, from tip of great toe to little toe.)	38 – 42 degrees	38 – 42 degrees

(a) As measured by podiatrists for 10 female and 10 male patients. Dr. Louise Robbins sampled 514 subjects. Both the podiatrist's aspect ratios and our ichnite aspect ratios for R-1 and R-2 fall within the minimum/maximum ranges of bare footprint measurements made by Dr. Robbins. The toe ratio R-3 and the toe taper angle may be innovations developed for this project. They add considerable credibility that these ichnites were indeed made by humans.

More literature research and measurements need to be completed to enhance the database for these aspects and to satisfy legitimate criticism.

(b) Eight ichnite samples were averaged.

(c) Aspect ratio formulas:

R-1 = Foot length divided by ball width.

R-2 = Ball width divided by heel width.

R-3 = Width of great toe divided by average width of other toes.

The obvious angle difference between the two tracks, previously shown in Figure 13, precludes them from being part of a single track impression.

Coffee Track

The discoverer's grandson, Mr. Fred Coffee, a member of the Stinnett City Council, is the current owner of the artifact. With his gracious cooperation the track was submitted to a nondestructive Spiral CT Scan analysis at a laboratory. While the information was being processed through the computer, the technical staff immediately pointed to the screen and emphasized the compression areas under the track and between the toes. The staff also emphasized the clearly discernible five toes, the three arches (medial, lateral, and metatarsal), and the overall distinctive shape of the human foot.

Attention was drawn to the depressions made by the dominant "great toe," the unique "second toe" that makes a slightly deeper depression, and the distinctive "ball" of the foot. When the analysis was complete the CT Scan had recorded the compression around the complete footprint, clearly indicating that the print was not carved or fabricated. In CT Scan X-rays, the lighter areas are more dense, since the X-rays have more difficulty traveling through that medium.

Figure C-33
Australian footprint from Willandra Lakes
District, 30 cm long   (S. Webb et al, 2006)

Figure C-34
Australian footprint from Willandra Lakes
District Photo released by Environment
Ministry   Michael Amendolia / AP Photo

Figure C-35
Trails of Australian footprints
Michael Amendolia / AP Photo

Figure 36
Austalian Footprint from Willandra Lakes
District (S. Webb et al, 2006 used by permission)

Figure C-36   Contour gage on cast of the Burdick track.

Figure C-37
Ryals track with detailed toe impression and color outline of track.

Figure C-38
Ryals track showing how toe drag marks match human foot.

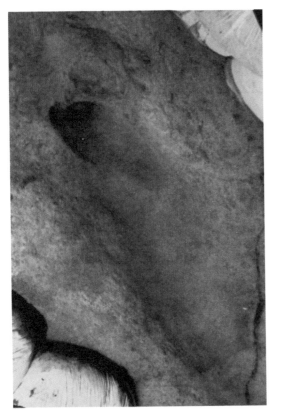

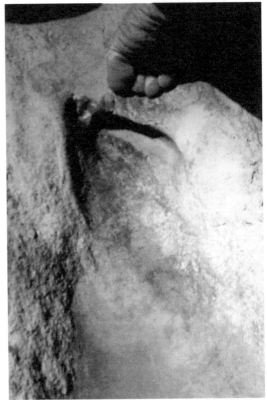

As it reaches the ground in forward locomotion the human foot first places pressure in the heel area, gently transfers the weight to the lateral longitudinal arch (creating a slight bulge in the upper outer section of the foot in the process), transfers the weight to the ball and the medial longitudinal arch, then transfers the weight to the metatarsal arch and the toes in a lifting motion.

Of significant importance is the fact that a thin crustal layer of sediment formed over the bulk rock as both layers lithified. The crustal layer followed the contour of the depression. This thin layer is clearly seen, since a section of it peeled off as Mr. Coffee was removing the artifact. Any carving activity would have cut through the outer layer, clearly leaving its evidence of fabrication

With these new technical data in hand we have come to the conclusion that the track is indeed genuine and is a depression left by the placement of a human foot while the matrix of "mud" was still fresh and pliable. All the professional academicians to whom the artifact has been shown rate it between 9.5 and 10.0 on a scale of 1 to 10.

Ref. (Baugh, Carl, www.Creationevidence. org, 2006)

Evaluation Criteria

Some general criteria have been established for evaluating human-like fossil footprints. From the December 1989 *CRS Quarterly* in the article on quasihuman, quasimammalian and dinosaur ichnofossils by Rosnau, Auldaney, Howe and Waisgerber, (Rosnau et al, 1989), the following criteria were listed.

1. The fossil print is within the size range of the foot of modern man

2. The print is shaped like a modern footprint.

3. The print is one of many of similar size

and shape.

4. The print is part of a trail or series of tracks that suggest a natural human gait or stride.

5. The print manifests some internal detail suggestive of human toes or shoe marks.

6. The print is bordered by mud that was squeezed out from under it as it was formed.

7. Fossil human bones and/or artifacts are known to exist within the same formation as the print.

It would seem reasonable to add to the first criterion "and authenticated fossil man". Some modern men have considerable stature and correspondingly large feet, but we do not want to rule out prints that might fit a fossil man yet undiscovered. The number 6 criterion lists the most desirable conditions, but the consistency of the medium and weight of the track maker produce a wide variation in print profiles without squeezing out mud. Look at what happens on new concrete.

It was stated along with the criteria that confirmation of between 3 and 7 of the criteria would provide a high confidence level for a human origin. Using these criteria with reference to the Clark and Taylor tracks, we find the following. They meet numbers 1 and 2, but number 3 does not apply to the Clark trail. For number 4 we have consistent paces, but the prevailing conditions did not provide a situation for "normal" walking. For number 5 there are some indication of toes, toe outlines and arches. Number 6 has limited correlation. If any of the fossil teeth are authenticated as human, then number 7 would be met, but as of the printing of this second edition this has not happened.

A statement by Dr. Gary Parker is also appropriate. "Footprints are more distinctive of man than most bone fragments are."(Parker and Morris, 1982, p. 126)

ANALYSIS OF TEETH

Note: Table 5, Definitions Used in Description of Teeth, is located at the end of this section on tooth analysis.

The discovery of an apparent human tooth on June 16, 1987 was an event that has caused considerable interest among creationists and among some evolutionists as well. Because it had been kept from air in the moist clay marl, it was well preserved. Reference Figures C-39 and C-40. Chemicals in the marl had caused it to become blackened as were the turtle bones found nearby in the same layer.

The approximate dimensions of the tooth are 7.9 mm wide at incisal edge, 5.6 mm wide at top of crown, 6.0 mm mesial height of crown and 4.0 mm distal height of crown. This is larger than average for modern deciduous incisors but still within the normal range.

The work of positively identifying it as either a human tooth or the tooth of some other creature continued for several years after the discovery. There is no doubt that it is a tooth. It has been so identified by dental experts including James Addison, DDS of Dallas, Kenneth Hogan, DMD of Fort Smith, Arkansas and by paleontologists Dr. Arthur Busby of the TCU paleontology department, Dr. Melissa Winoms of the Texas University Balcones vertebrate paleontology laboratory, Dr. Charles Finsley of the Dallas Museum of Natural History and Dr. Raymond Purdy, Curator of Vertebrate Paleontology at the Smithsonian Institute in Washington, D.C.

The fact that dentists, upon seeing either the tooth or detailed photographs of it, could immediately identify it as a deciduous maxillary right central incisor caused some of the paleontologists to ask the question "What do dentists know about teeth?" It has been learned from several dentists that one of the basic courses for beginning dental students is one in which they must make both drawings and carvings of human teeth. Dental textbooks, such as *Dental Anatomy* by Julian B. Woelfel, (Woelfel, Julian B., 1984) provide a good illustration of the kind of detailed understanding required of dental students. And in their dental practice they see teeth on a daily basis. The characteristics of this tooth were in agreement with those stated in Table 4, Characteristics of Deciduous Teeth.

Initial reactions of paleontologists upon learning that the tooth had been found in Cretaceous limestone was to state that it was a fish tooth, either from a Pycnodont, an extinct fossil form found in Cretaceous limestone in Texas and Mississippi, or a Sargodon, a supposed ancestor of the modern day sheepshead. The Pycnodont had incisor type teeth as shown in Figure 37, but only when severely worn to the point of eliminating the groove in the incisal edge would it begin to appear similar to a human incisor.

Sargodon teeth, when viewed from the side, have an appearance similar to human teeth, but an overall comparison shows a number of differences. None of the photographs or fossil samples of fish teeth seen by the Task Force have yet produced a comparison to the physical characteristics of the Glen Rose tooth. This includes the photos of Ron Hastings' pycnodont teeth that have some

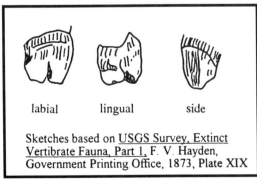

labial   lingual   side

Sketches based on USGS Survey, Extinct Vertibrate Fauna, Part 1, F. V. Hayden, Government Printing Office, 1873, Plate XIX

Figure 37 Pycnodont Tooth Characteristics

similarities to the Glen Rose tooth, but careful examination of the photos indicates some distinct differences as well. Figure 38, a set of sketches based on photographs, shows a comparison of the Glen Rose tooth and a Pycnodont tooth. The similarities between the pycnodont and the Glen Rose teeth are:

> size
> color
> smooth labial surface
> crown wider than long

Differences noted from the available photos include:

Pycnodont incisal edge has a pronounced indentation whereas the Glen Rose tooth (and human deciduous incisors) has a continuous edge, i.e., no mamelons.

The cingulum in the fish tooth is deeper than in the Glen Rose tooth.

The cervix in the fish tooth is not as pronounced as in the Glen Rose tooth.

The fish tooth crown does not appear bulbous as does the Glen Rose tooth, a characteristic of human deciduous incisors.

The top view of the fish tooth is teardrop shaped, and the Glen Rose tooth top view is oval, common to human teeth.

The poor quality of available pycnodont teeth photos did not permit their reproduction here.

Another difference between human and pycnodont teeth is that human teeth have roots, but pycnodont teeth are mounted on pedicles (small posts).

One type of analysis that was done on the tooth was a SEM analysis of the tooth surface, looking for the distinctive pattern that often shows up in human tooth enamel. Figure 39 is a photograph of the type of pattern being looked for. This analysis was first done by Dr. David Menton, a microscopic anatomist at Washington University Medical School. Dr. Menton's results are as stated in a letter to Paul Bartz. (Menton, David, 1987)

"I compared the acid-etched surface of the Glen Rose fossil tooth with that of a human deciduous incisor and an incisor form tooth of the salt water sheepshead fish of the genus Sargus (neither of the latter two were fossils). The purpose of this study was to determine whether the Glen Rose tooth most closely resembles the human tooth with which it has been compared or a fish tooth of the type found in a fossil Sargodon. Regrettably, I did not have a Sargodon tooth at my disposal so I used a marginal incisorform tooth from Sargus after which I understand the fossil genus Sargodon was named by reason of their similarity. The results are in my view unambiguous, the Glen Rose tooth has virtually none of the microscopic features one would reasonably expect of mammalian enamel. Specifically, it lacks any suggestion of enamel prisms and instead has a woven fibrous appearance of a type not found in any true enamel but typical of the durodentin that covers most of the exposed surface of fish teeth. The Glen Rose tooth and that of Sargus, on the other hand, were far more similar to each other than either were to the human tooth."

The result of Dr. Menton's analysis was at first a cause for concern since all other indications were that the tooth more closely resembled a human tooth rather than a fish tooth. Research into dental reports and texts soon provided more information relative to the SEM analysis. From the book *Oral Histology: Development, Structure, and Function* (Ten Cate, A. R., no date) it was

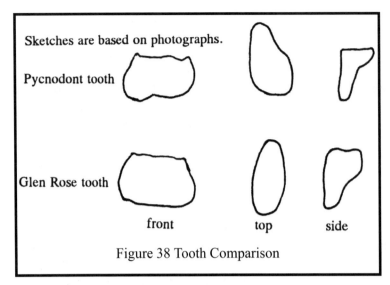

Sketches are based on photographs.

Pycnodont tooth

Glen Rose tooth

front   top   side

Figure 38 Tooth Comparison

Dentistry, Dallas, Texas. Dr. McIntosh considered the tooth genuinely human based on the morphology (features comprised in the form and structure) that matches 10 for 10 basic characteristics of a human tooth. The comparison of the physical features is shown in Table 3. Dr. McIntosh concluded that dentists would not confuse this tooth with known samples of fish teeth, either modern or extinct, and stated so in a meeting of the Metroplex Institute for Origins Science. Examination of the internal structure of the tooth disclosed characteristics similar to a human tooth with the enamel to dentin ratio being in the range of modern adult human teeth.

learned that not all deciduous teeth have the distinctive rod pattern. Photographs in the book on pages 214 & 215 of the second edition show several patterns of tooth enamel from deciduous teeth, one of which closely resembles the pattern found by Dr. Menton in the Glen Rose tooth. It was also found from experimenting with modern deciduous teeth and from dental reports that deeper etching of the enamel of deciduous teeth is required to see the enamel pattern. On this basis, it was considered possible that Dr. Menton's conclusions as stated in his letter to Paul Bartz might have been premature.

Additional analysis of the tooth was done by Dr. James McIntosh, professor of anatomy and histology at the Baylor School of

A lingual surface wear facet was identified by Dr. Paul Goaz, also of Baylor School of Dentistry. Figure 40 is a sketch showing the wear facet location. This feature is only made by the grinding of an opposing incisor

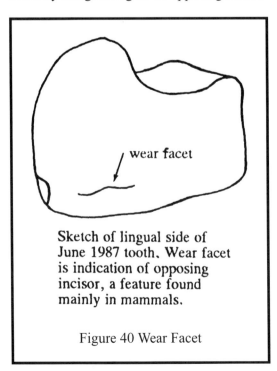

wear facet

Sketch of lingual side of June 1987 tooth. Wear facet is indication of opposing incisor, a feature found mainly in mammals.

Figure 40 Wear Facet

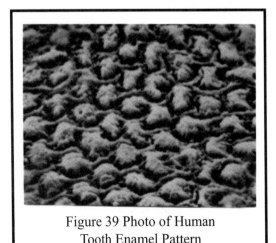

Figure 39 Photo of Human
Tooth Enamel Pattern

TEXAS TRACKS and ARTIFACTS

according to Dr. Goaz. Opposing crown contact only occurs in mammals and a few dinosaurs with a different type of teeth. (Peyer, B., 1968)

Examination of the enamel microstructure of the tooth by Dr. McIntosh produced results different from those obtained by Dr. Menton. However, the characteristics were not the same as observed in modern teeth, even when taking into account the basic variations documented in dental texts. Instead of the keyhole rod pattern, there was a tubular structure.

Comparison was made with other enamel patterns, and it was found that the closest match was to a modern sheepshead fish enamel pattern although there are noted differences between the two as shown in Figure 41. It appeared that what was found was a tooth that was physically identical to a modern deciduous incisor except for one characteristic, the enamel structure. Dr. Petra Wilder-Smith had researched the literature for comparative microstructure, but did not identify any.

A small sample of material was taken from the Glen Rose tooth and used to conduct a radio-immuno assay test, a test of the genetic material in the tooth. This was

done at San Francisco State University. The test results showed comparison to mammals (human, chimpanzee and horse) but not to fish (trout). Numerical values obtained in the test were lower than needed for a positive identification. The sample used in the test was taken from the root canal and was contaminated with clay. Because of the time

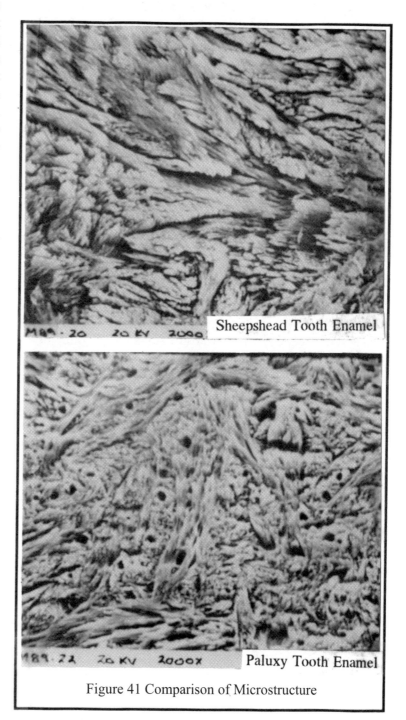

Figure 41 Comparison of Microstructure

87

and money required to conduct this type of test, it has not been repeated.

One other comparison was yet to be made. Several teeth were removed from the fossil skeleton of Moab Man, a skeleton that had been removed from between rock layers in Utah and which possibly has had some similar aging effects as the Glen Rose tooth. The enamel pattern in the Moab man teeth matched modern enamel patterns, thus apparently ruling out a change in the enamel due to long burial.

The present conclusion is that the tooth is of unknown origin since its distinctive human features with a fish-like enamel structure have not previously been documented.

As stated earlier, the tooth was found in clay marl between two layers of limestone and was well protected from weathering. It was black in color and consisted only of the crown. A fracture line on the front surface further indicates that the tooth may have been violently separated from its owner.

The second tooth, found along the Paluxy River on August 18, 1992 is shown in Figure C-41 as it was found attached to the limestone rock. It had the following measurements, taken by Gorman Gray.

Width of incisal edge	0.350 inches
Mesial height	0.354 inches
Distal height	0.294 inches
Width of crown-top	0.268 inches

A darker area of the tooth above the cervix is shown in Figure C-39. The distance from the incisal edge to the dark band was 0.239 inch on the mesial side and 0.230 inch on the distal side.

When the tooth was removed from the rock matrix, additional photos were taken to document the contours. Dr. Baugh gave the following brief description of the tooth:

Upper left central incisor with organic remnants in the crown.

Contains crown, portion of root, cingula,

cisal edge wear facet, mesial wear facet, distal wear facet.

(preliminary observation: some human teeth show identical wear facets) Shape is a lens section.

On August 22nd, a local dentist observed the tooth and stated that it appeared to be a human tooth. What were initially identified as mesial and distal wear facets were actually small chips according to the dentist. The wear on the incisal edge indicates a person about 40 years of age by modern standards. It probably came from a relatively small person because of its size and shape.

The enamel pattern of the second tooth was examined and found to be similar to that of the first tooth. Two of a kind may only be a coincidence, but it could also be the beginning of a trend. When the third tooth was found, we had to wait some months to find out if the trend was a reality. Dr. McIntosh found that the enamel pattern was essentially the same as in the first two teeth and so a trend has been established.

The third tooth (reference Figure C-43) was smaller than the first two but still within the size range of human teeth. Width of the crown is approximately 5.5 mm at the incisal edge and 4.0 mm at the cervix. Crown height is 3 mm, and overall height is 6 mm that includes a significant amount of root structure.

Table 6, Tooth Crown Size Comparison, shows the basic dimensions of the crowns of the three fossil teeth.

Table 6
Tooth Crown Size Comparison in mm

	1	2	3
Width, incisal edge	7.9	8.9	5.5
Width, crown top	5.6	6.8	4.0
Mesial height	6.0	6.1	3.0
Distal height	4.0	5.8	2.6

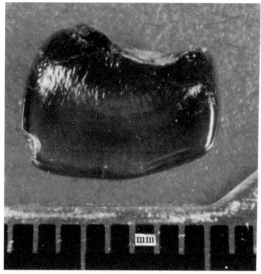

Figure C-39
Fossil tooth, 1987, lingual

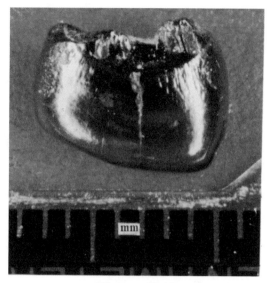

Figure C-40
Fossil tooth, 1987, labial

Figure C-41
Second tooth as
found, attached to
limestone

Figure C-40
Third tooth -
labial

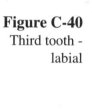
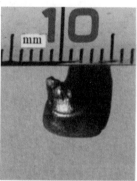

Figure C-42
Second tooth
showing size

Figure C-44
Third tooth -
lingual

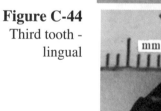

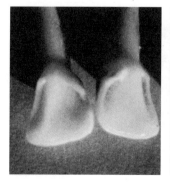
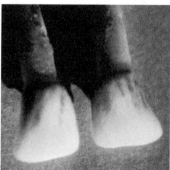

Figure C-45 (Left)
Deer teeth, lower jaw incisors.
Deer have no upper front teeth.

Figure C-46 (Right)
Deer teeth, lower jaw incisors.

Figure C-47
Small fossil insect. Actual size approx. .05"

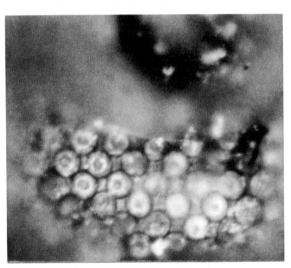

Figure C-48
Enlargement of insect eye, 400X

Figure C-49
Sketch of Kuban core details based on photograph.   Infilling is shown as dark color internal to the cores that coincides with the rust colored surface area.   Colors in sketch do not represent actual core colors.

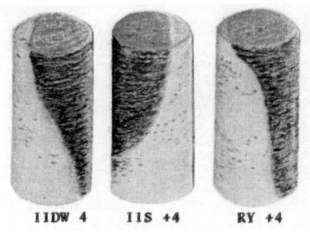

It was suggested that a comparison be made between the fossil teeth and deer teeth. A number of hunters were questioned about front incisors from white tail deer that are the most common in the Midwest. It seems that hunters don't check the teeth. In order to obtain samples of deer teeth, several hunters were asked to provide some if they had any hunting success. A visit was also made to a deer processing facility during hunting season where a number of deer heads were checked. To our surprise we found that white tail deer have lower incisors but no upper incisors, in fact, no upper front teeth. This configuration is also found in cattle.

Two sets of deer lower teeth were obtained from the deer processing facility and two from hunters. The central incisors were removed from one jawbone for a determination of the root structure and of the transition region between the crown and the root. Figures C-45 and C-46 are the lingual and labial views, respectively, of the removed teeth.

The crowns of the deer central incisors are about the same size as the crowns of human incisors, but there are two distinct differences in structure. Human incisors have a pronounced cingulum, a bulge on the cervical third of the lingual surface. The three fossil incisors found along the Paluxy River have definite cingula. Deer teeth have a concave, shovel like lingual surface with a small ridge paralleling the distal edge. The second difference is in the taper of the crown. Using the fossil teeth crown measurements, the ratio of the width of the incisal edge to the width of the crown top falls between 1.31 and 1.41. The same ratio from four deer teeth falls between 1.78 and 1.92.

It appears that deer lower incisors are enough different from human upper incisors and from the fossil teeth to rule out the possibility of the fossil teeth being from deer.

The roots of the first two fossil teeth had apparently been broken off. In speculating about a common reason in keeping with the flood scenario, it was assumed that if the victims who lost the teeth were floating face down in shallow water, wave action could produce a bobbing effect in which the front teeth would strike against the surface over which the water was flowing. Eventually, this would result in fracturing the tooth. It is also a possibility that the body from which the tooth came could be in the same vicinity, but since most of the rock strata are under ground, finding it would be unlikely.

Another factor to be considered in understanding the difficulty in finding a complete human skeleton with teeth intact is that corpses tend to float and disarticulate so are rarely buried quickly for fossilization to occur. This conclusion is based on taphanomic studies of floating mammal corpses. Also, the durability of teeth allows them to survive although they tend to become scattered because they gradually fall out of skulls as the alveoli decays. (Woodmorappe, John, 1983) Such teeth would probably not have broken roots, as did those found in the Glen Rose strata.

What have we learned from this analysis? Based on morphology the teeth look very human according to numerous dentists. But enamel patterns appear similar to known fish teeth enamel. Is there some unidentified fish that has human-like teeth? Or is there some pre-flood branch of human beings that had a different enamel pattern on their teeth? More information is needed to solve this puzzling situation.

Table 3
CHARACTERISTICS OF DECIDUOUS TEETH

All Deciduous Teeth:

Shorter crowns than in permanent teeth

Enamel bulges at cervical line rather than gradual tapering

Crowns appear bulbous

Usually no depressions on labial surface of crown of incisors, surfaces are smooth

Cervical ridge on the facial surface is prominent

No mamelons on the incisal edge

Cingulums are prominent (bulge) and occupy about 1/3 of crown length

Deciduous Maxillary Central Incisors:

Crown is wider than it is long

Crown narrows at the cervix

Incisal edge is quite flat except for some rounding at the disto-incisal edge (side next to lateral incisor)

Labial surface is smooth

Mesial side of the crown is fairly flat, distal side is more convex

Table 4
Comparison of Tooth Characteristics

Identified Characteristics of Deciduous Incisors	1987 Tooth
1. The crowns have a marked constriction at the cervix.	Yes
2. The crowns appear bulbous, often having labial or bucccal cincula.	Yes
3. There are no mamelons on the incisal edge.	Yes
4. The cingula are prominent or seem to bulge and occupy about one-third of the cervicoincisal length.	Yes
5. The crown is wider than it is long, but is narrow near the cervix.	Yes
6. The incisal edge is quite flat except for some rounding at the distoincisal angle.	Yes
7. The labial surface is smooth; usually there are no depressions.	Yes
8. The mesial side of the crown is fairly flat, whereas the distal side is more convex.	Yes
9. The marginal ridges are often distinct and prominent.	Yes
10. The curvature of the cervical line is greater on the mesial than on the distal surface.	Yes

NOTE: Basic characteristics are as listed by Don Patton in a lecture at a Twin Cities Creation Science Association meeting, Nov. 15, 1988, Roseville, MN

TABLE 5
DEFINITIONS USED IN DESCRIPTION OF TEETH
(Woelfel, 1984)

Cervix - The part of the root near the cementoenamel junction.

Cervical line - Cementoenamel junction

Cervical ridge - A ridge running mesiodistally on the cervical one-third of the buccal surface of the crown. Found on all deciduous teeth, but only on permanent molars.

Cingulum - The enlargement or bulge on the cervical third of the lingual surface of the crown in incisors and canines.

Crown - The part of the tooth that has an enamel surface.

Dentin - The hard tissue underlying enamel and cementum and making up the bulk of the tooth.

Distal - Away from the midline of the dental arch.

Incisal edge - The cutting edge or surface of incisors.

Labial surface - The surface of anterior teeth nearest the lips.

Lingual surface - The surface of teeth nearest the tongue.

Mamelon - One of three tubercles sometimes present on the incisal edge of an incisor tooth that has not been subject to wear.

Maxillary - The upper teeth.

Mesial - Toward the centerline of the dental arch: i.e. toward the plane between the right and left central incisors.

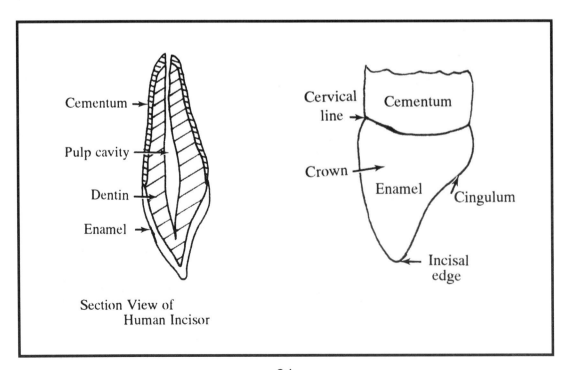

Cementum

Pulp cavity

Dentin

Enamel

Section View of
Human Incisor

Cervical line

Cementum

Crown

Enamel

Cingulum

Incisal edge

Analysis of the Finger

The finding of the fossil "finger" was an undocumented event. Because of the time lapse between when it was found and when it came into Dr. Carl Baugh's possession, it precluded finding any associated material. It is a classic example of circumstantial evidence.

What is the probability that this piece of limestone is actually a fossil finger? And if it is, how can a flesh form be fossilized? Fossilization requires rapid burial before decomposition and disintegration occur. The material covering the object subject to fossilization must be firm enough to retain its shape during the fossilization process. Mammal bones are often found, but seldom can flesh forms be found because the conditions for such fossilization seldom occur. But they do occur.

The Paluxy limestone beds and adjacent limestone deposits are evidence for rapid strata formation, contrary to information found in brochures which state that they were formed over thousands of years. The tracks impressed in the soft mud which quickly hardened into rock layers and the fossil clams, which in some cases left a void in the rock surface as they escaped from the hardening mud, are but several evidences of a rapid formation of a complete layer at one time. The material was also firm enough to retain the shape of an object embedded in it.

A human body washed into a mud slurry while it was still being deposited would be mostly covered with mud. Even if the main part of the body tended to float, the arm and hand would more likely be encased in the mud. Relatively rapid hardening of the mud would leave the flesh encased in a rigid conformal coating of rock so that, as the body decomposed, it would gradually become filled with limestone by the process of cellular decomposition replacement. The bone may have been partially decomposed. X-ray analysis of the finger did not reveal any internal structure because of the density of the limestone and its similarity to bone. Magnetic imaging tests were also negative. A later Cat-scan revealed internal details.

Physical comparison of the finger profile compared to a live human finger profile is shown in Figure 42. Both profiles are approximately actual size. The minor additional details on the live finger such as the fingernail extension and the small skin creases on the top of the finger set it apart from the fossil. The general shape and size indicate that the fossil is very likely a genuine reproduction of a finger of a flood victim. To further verify this conclusion, the finger was sawed diagonally as shown in Figure C-50 to reveal any internal structure. Figure C-51 shows the details found. The skin layer was clearly identifiable around most of the periphery. The bone surface is also quite distinct in some areas when examining the fossil although photographic reproduction

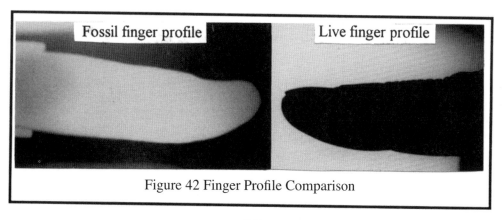

Fossil finger profile | Live finger profile

Figure 42 Finger Profile Comparison

does not show all the details. Bone marrow is a different color from the rest of the fossil. Flesh around the bone is in proportion to a normal finger, being thicker on the bottom (palm side). The two round spots, one near the top and the other below it near the bottom, are the tendons. The difference in size corresponds to actual tendons with the stronger one at the bottom providing strength for grasping objects. The tendons were identified by the cat scan of the fossil which revealed the bone, fingernail root, tendons and other details. This verification of the structure as being the same as a normal finger seems to give sufficient proof of its authenticity.

The sectioned fossil was shown to sixteen medical doctors at a single display. It was reported that all verified the features to be identical to those of the human phalanges. Dr. Dale Peterson from Edmond, Oklahoma had seen the fossil before it was sectioned. He stated that it looked like a human finger. After the fossil had been sectioned he viewed it again. "At that time I observed that the fossil was not of uniform or random density and coloration. The internal appearance of the fossil was identical to what one sees when a human finger is sectioned. The skin margins and subcutaneous tissue were clearly delineated. The bone matrix was clearly defined, and features consistent with flexor and extensor tendons were present. ... It is my professional opinion that the fossil unearthed at Glen Rose, Texas is, in fact, a petrified human finger and not an infill of a wormhole or similar artifact." (Peterson, Dale H., 2002)

What is the probability that a piece of limestone rock could form in the shape of a human finger, with fingernail, without a form or mold to shape the pattern? Statistically, it would be an unlikely event. But fossilization of flesh forms is not uncommon in Somervell County since this county is known to paleontology for its "perfect" fossilized worms.

There are those who would argue that the fossil finger is nothing more than an odd-shaped piece of limestone. This type of circumstantial evidence is more likely rejected on a philosophical basis because of where it was found rather than on a technical basis because of what it appears to be.

Figure C-50
Fossil finger showing sectioning cuts.

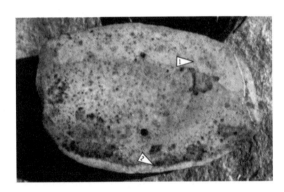

Figure C-51
Enlarged view of section showing 1) bone/flesh boundary and 2) skin/flesh boundary.

Part III
SUPPLEMENT ON METAL HAMMER ARTIFACT

Background

The hammer artifact was first discovered by Mr. and Mrs. Max Hahn of London, Texas in June 1936. It was found near London, Texas on the bank of the Llano River near the mouth of Red Creek. Only a portion of the wooden handle was exposed from the rock when it was found, the hammerhead being totally encased. The original identification of the rock type was Ordovician, but later analysis of the area by geologist John Watson showed it to be basal Cretaceous concretionary sandstone (Hensell Sand Formation). Orthodox dating places this ledge near to 135 MYBP. Figure 43 is a sketch of the location where the hammer was found.

In 1946/47, the rock encasing the artifact was broken open by Max Hahn's son George Hahn, thus exposing the metal hammer. Observations showed that the hammer was approximately 60 percent exposed on one side with the rock tightly formed around it. Although initially the metal showed little if any signs of oxidation, an amount of rust has now formed. Originally its appearance was relatively smooth with a brownish fossil coating. Today it is somewhat rough in comparison. The hammer has also loosened up from the rock since it was first exposed. Figures C-52, C-53, C-54 and C-55 are photos of the hammer partially exposed in the rock.

Description and Discussion of the Hammer

The hammerhead is rectangular in shape with the working ends of different design. One end has a + shaped configuration, and the other has a protrusion that could possibly be an insert. The photos show these details.

Mr. Roland Wardell, a metallurgical historian, looked at the photos of the hammer to determine what information he could provide in respect to analyzing the metal content and construction. The hammer could be X-rayed. This would reveal some stringer like inclusions if it were wrought iron, an indication of primitive technology. It would also provide information about the rusty appearing end. Mr. Wardell suggested that it may have been a marking hammer, but others have suggested that it was a metal working hammer with some other material (wood or leather) having originally been placed around the protrusion at the one end. This material had subsequently decayed, leaving a void in that area.

Preliminary material identification was performed at Battelle Labs in Columbus, Ohio with the following results:

Area No. 1 Iron 96.6%, Chlorine 2.6%, Sulfur 0.74%
Area No. 2 Iron, Chlorine, Sulfur, Silicon

Results of this test are considered preliminary and are kept in a safe deposit box by the Creation Evidence Museum. No formal report was written of the analysis.

Several methods of non-destructive surface testing have been considered. By using the Scanning Electron Microscope (SEM), either Energy Dispersive Spectroscopy (EDS) or Wavelength Dispersive Spectroscopy (WDS) could be used. These methods require a smooth surface to obtain accurate quantitative information. The hammer does not appear to be a suitable sample for this type of analysis. There may also be contaminants on the surface that will produce results that are not representative of the main body of the hammer. A small sample from within the hammer would be needed to conduct a destructive analysis if quantitative results are desired.

Suggestions have been made that the hammer is possibly made from meteorite material. Meteorite iron is known to contain significant amounts of nickel, and this could be easily verified by an EDS spectrum analysis. Since nickel did not show on the preliminary material analysis, it is doubtful that the metal had a meteoritic origin.

Claims have also been made that the rock encasing the hammer is infilled material. Mr. Philip Isett, a soil scientist, has examined the rock and stated that it is not infilled material. The rock surrounding the hammer is a concretion. However, the entire area in which it was found is concretionary sandstone.

The wooden handle of the hammer has not been identified as to type, but it appears to be similar to modern hammer handles made from ash or hickory. The wood is not fossilized, although portions adjacent to the hammerhead are coalified. No radio carbon dating of the wood has been conducted.

Question for consideration:

What kind of evidences do the science disciplines cite for identifying re-deposited material, and how successful does this identification perform in a blind analysis?

Recommendations

1. X-ray the hammer for baseline information and see if the smelting resembles wrought iron with stringer-like inclusions. This would also show any irregularities.
2. Take a small sample of metal away from the surface of the hammer and identify the location.
   A. Perform an EDS analysis for identification of elements.
   B. Perform a quantitative analysis using a destructive type test.

Later Analysis

In August 1992, a tomographic analysis of the hammer was conducted at Texas Utilities.

A reprint of one of the pictures taken at that time is shown in Figure C-56. A verbal report identified the hammer material as being of superior quality with no inclusions or irregularities in its composition. The protrusion on one end was an integral part of the metal. Surface density was indicated to be a uniform 6 percent greater than the interior of the metal. This evidence of quality fabrication is an indication of high technology metallurgy. Additional testing was conducted in 2002.

Hammer Reexamined

Summary, July 2002

Based on the analysis and test results, the hammer was found genuinely encased by limonite and goethite mineralization where it underwent many years of *in situ* corrosion and degradation from contact with acidic groundwater containing sulfur and chlorine salts. The corrosive environment became active during cycles of wetness as indicated by concentric layering of iron oxide and other corrosion products.
The hammer head was composed of a wrought, hardened and plain medium-carbon steel whose chemical composition and shape resembled, but did not fit, known American hammer steels in recent striking tool standards. (Stolk, Douglas A., 2002)

The Energy Dispersive X-Ray Spectroscopy Results

The semi-quantitative results are from drill chips obtained by drilling a 1/16-inch diameter hole to depths of 0.05 and 0.125 inches. The chip test results are shown in the table below compared to the results obtained from the original testing done by Battelle Labs.

The recent test results differ with those reported from the original analysis, but it should be noted that both sulfur and chlorine are corrosive to steel in the presence of environmental moisture. Any amount of

| | Percent Composition | | |
	0.05 chip	0.125 chip	Original
Aluminum	0.37	--	--
Silicon	0.16	0.17	--
Chlorine	0.11	--	2.6
Iron	99.20	99.63	96.6
Manganese	0.15	0.20	--
Sulfur	--	--	0.74

corrosion material in the test sample will affect the results.

The results obtained from testing corrosion products from initial drilling (close to the surface) show the following results:

Carbon 10.09%, Oxygen 30.33%, Aluminum 0.32%, Silicon 0.46%, Sulfur 0.76%, Chlorine 0.29%, Calcium 0.57%, Iron 56.95%, Manganese 0.23%

According to the report of the retesting, the corrosion on the surface of the hammer varied so that test result also varied accordingly. Since much of the corrosion was produced during wet conditions in the rock encasing the hammer, and the corrosion was found in thin layers, this is an indication of aging. (Stolk, Douglas A., 2002) The hammer is not a recently lost miner's tool.

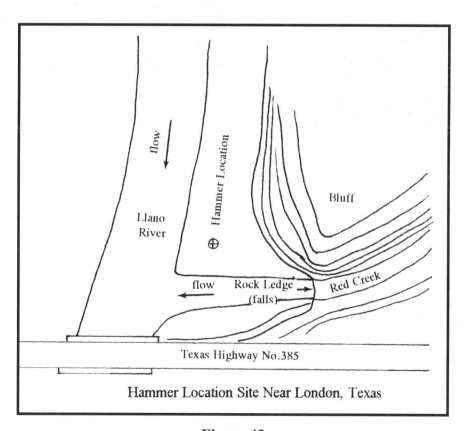

Figure 43
Hammer Location site
near London, TX

Figure C-52
Hammer found near London, TX - 1936.
Rock encasing the hammer is Cretaceous
concretionary-sandstone. It was broken
open to expose the hammer.

Figure C-55
Enlarged view of end
with + configuration.

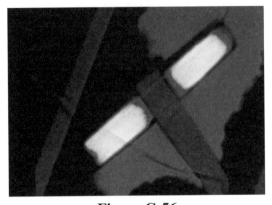

Figure C-56
False color print from Tomographic X-ray of
hammer. Pink area around hammer is rock.
There were no inclusions or irregularities in
the metal, indicating advanced metallurgy.
Protrusion at end was part of hammer metal,
not an insert.

Figure C-53
Alternate view of hammer with
+ end configuration on right.

Figure C-54
Details of end with protrusion
that may have had
other material around it.

Figure 44
Newspaper Rock Figure
(Approximate sketch)

PART IV SUPPORTING EVIDENCES

While the footprints of men and dinosaurs together in the same rock stratum gets a significant amount of attention, there are other types of evidence which support the claim that men and dinosaurs co-existed in historical time.

ARTIFACTS

Man's ability to produce works of art in a variety of mediums has shown his creativity and his appreciation of details in the world of nature that God has created. Some of that artwork deals with animals, and included in the animal types are figures of dinosaurs.

Petroglyphs and pictographs

Petroglyph identification is simplified when one understands the way creatures are usually represented.

Birds are represented as seen in flight and observed from below.

Animals and people are represented as seen standing or walking.

Fish and amphibians are represented as seen from above.

One of the well-known dinosaur petroglyph figures located in the Grand Canyon is shown in Figure C-57.

Another well-known pictograph location is in Lake Superior Provincial Park on the east shore of Lake Superior in Ontario, Canada. Agawa Rock paintings in the park are listed as Ojibwa Indian Art. One of the main figures is that of a large four-legged animal having two large curved horns on its head, a long tail, and spikes running from the neck to the end of the tail. See Figure C-58. Associated with this creature are other pictographs of two serpents and a canoe containing four or five people.

Newspaper Rock in Utah has numerous petroglyph figures of animals and people. One of the figures portrayed as a large aquatic creature has four legs, a long tail and a long neck. The head has two large curved horns similar to the horns in the pictograph figure in Canada.

The difference in presentation, one aquatic and one land animal, poses the possibility that the same type of creature is being represented but in two different environments. Figure 44, is a sketch based on the Newspaper Rock figure.

A dinosaur pictograph is found near Blanding, Utah at Natural Bridges State Park. Artwork associated with the Anasazi culture is located underneath one of the bridges in White Rock Canyon. See Figure C-59.

Effigy Mounds

Early residents of North America made outline replicas of people, birds and animals in the form of raised earthen mounds. At one time over 20,000 effigy mounds were identified in the three Midwest states of Minnesota, Wisconsin and Iowa. Their age has been determined to be from 1000 to 2000 years old. Most mounds no longer exist because of farming. But due to the foresight of civil engineer Alfred Hill with the help of archaeologist Theodore Lewis the mounds in the Midwest were found, measured and documented over the period from 1880 to 1910. Their 30 survey documents on microfilm are available at the Historical Museum of Minnesota in St. Paul.

Some of those mounds depict features that we associate with dinosaurs. Identification of animal types in the effigy mounds follows the same guidelines as listed for Petroglyphs.
Russell McGlenn studied the microfilm documents and made hundreds of sketches of different mound figures. (McGlenn, Russell, 1996)

Three effigy figures are shown in Figure 45 along with the dinosaur types they possibly represent. They are the Apatosaurus, Ankylosaurus and either a Centrosaurus or an Eoceratops.

Pottery

Pottery has historically been a medium where artists have used animal replicas as the basis for shaping or adorning a particular piece. People who knew dinosaurs were no different. The Mexican pitcher from about 1200 AD, and shown in Figure C-61, has a dinosaur shaped handle.

From the same area come hundreds (thousands) of ceramic figurines of various animal types including dinosaurs. It is obvious that the persons making the replicas had living animals as models for their handiwork. Museo Waldemar Julsrud in Acambaro, Mexico has hundreds of figurines on display. Fig. C-62 is one example. The time period for the creation of these figurines is from 800 BC to 200 AD.

The Moche culture of Peru made beautiful vases of a unique design that were decorated with images of dinosaurs and people. Dr. Dennis Swift has documented a number of these vases in his book *Secrets of the Ica Stones and Nazca Lines.* (Swift, Dennis, 2006) Figure C-60 is a typical Moche vase. Additional vases can be seen on www.creationism.org or www.dinosaursandman.com.

Burial Stones

Burial stones from Peru have been mentioned in history for many years, more as a curiosity because of their use in mortuary practices. These engraved stones depict a variety of figures, many of which are dinosaurs. The different types of dinosaurs are easily recognized. They are often shown in association with people.

Shown in Figure C-66 is a stone from a cemetery in the Nazca Valley south of Ica, Peru. Here a mixture of Nazca and Ica graves date from 400AD to 1000 AD. The scale of the man is disproportionate in size to that of the dinosaur, but consistent with the figures on pre-Columbian pottery of the Moche, Wari and Nazca of Peru.

Shown in Figure C-63 is another burial stone with three dinosaurs. The details engraved on these figures are evidence of personal familiarity with the animals, a direct indication of coexistence of men and dinosaurs.

Temple Carvings

An elaborately carved temple in Cambodia has figures of numerous creatures adorning its stone columns. One of the figures is that of a stegosaur with detailed "plates" on its back. This temple dates from 1200 AD. The artists involved with the carvings were evidently familiar with their subjects based on the details shown in their work, Figure C-65

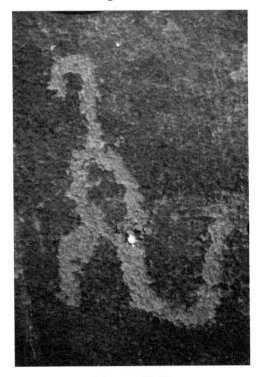

Figure C-57
Dinosaur petroglyph from Grand Canyon

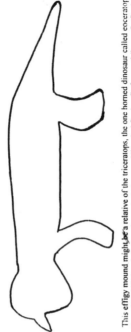

This effigy mound might be a relative of the triceratops, the one horned dinosaur called eoceratops. From The Hill/Lewis Survey Journals, Minnesota Historical Society Reference Library, St. Paul. Minnesota, unpublished microfilm.

I believe this effigy is a stylized representation of an apatosaurus as viewed from the side with its long neck and tail emphasized. The article in American Antiquarian, March. 1889 p. 78. says this is a turtle. I believe this is wrong, for the Indian classification system would always show an aquatic animal as viewed from the top. This is a land animal because it is pictured from the side

Effigy mound drawings compared to animal types that the mounds possibly were made to represent.

1. Apatosaurus
2. Ankylosaurus
3. Eoceratops or Centrosaurus

Figure 45 Effigy Mound Figures

Figure C-58
Agawa Rock pictographs, Ontario, Canada

Figure C-59
Natural Bridges Dinosaur

Figure C-60
Moche vase, Peru

Figure C-61
Mexican pitcher, circa 1200 AD

Figure C-63
Ica burial stone, Peru

Figure 62
Dinosaur figurine, Acambaro, Mexico

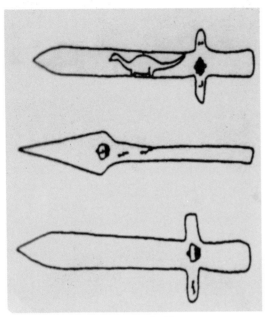

Figure C-64

Tucson Artifacts, Arizona, circa 850 AD

Figure C-66

Ica burial stone, circa 1000 AD, Peru

Figure C-65

Cambodian Temple carving of Stegosaur, 1200 AD

Figure C-67

Roman Mosaic, 3rd century AD, Israel

MISCELLANEOUS ART WORKS

Mosaics

Decorations of mosaic art are seen in many buildings, both ancient and modern. One of particular interest is a mosaic showing a man and dinosaur. See Figure C-67. It is located in the remains of a Roman mansion at Sapphori, Israel and dated to the third century AD. The modern discovery of the mosaic was in 1987 by Eric and Carol Meyer of Duke University. The Israel Department of Antiquities performed (supervised) the excavation.

Ceremonial pieces

The "Tucson Artifacts" are lead objects made in the form of crosses, spears, swords and arrows. Some of the objects have engraved figures, one of which is the shape of a dinosaur.

Ref. Figure C-64 This Apatasaurus type dinosaur is shown with the tail raised, a position recently recognized as correct. This is further evidence that the person making the engraving was familiar with the animal.

The earliest mention of these objects dates back to about 1880. Numerous articles were uncovered in the 1920s by Thomas W. Bent and Charles E. Manier. A hard coating of caliche on the objects indicated that they had been buried for hundreds of years. Inscriptions led to the conclusion that these objects had a Roman origin dating back to the period of 775 – 900 AD during a Jewish-Roman occupation of the area. .

Analysis of the artifacts by professionals convinced many of their authenticity, but the charges of fraud by the Smithsonian caused considerable controversy. (Koenig, Earl, 2000)

HISTORY RECORDS

Biblical References

Most people familiar with the Bible recognize the names Behemoth and Leviathan from the book of Job, chapters 40 and 41. Behemoth is described as a large land animal with characteristics fitting a number of large dinosaurs. Leviathan is described as a large amphibian with dinosaurian characteristics.

Publications

After the Flood, **The early post-flood history of Europe traced back to Noah** by Bill Cooper, New Wine Press, 1995

In Chapter 10 of this book titled **Dinosaurs from Anglo-Saxon and other Records**, and Chapter 11, ***Beowulf and the Creatures of Denmark***, Cooper provides answers to the often-asked questions about dinosaurs in the early history records. He cites references dating from 300 BC to modern times of encounters with land creatures, water creatures and flying reptiles.

Man, Dinosaurs and Mammals Together by John Allen Watson, Mt. Blanco Publishing Co., 2001

This book is a summary of the evidence from the phosphate rocks/bone phosphates of South Carolina. Watson lists land mammals, marine mammals, reptiles (including dinosaurs), fish and marine life, and human bones and artifacts found together in these beds.

Secular references

The name "Loch Ness monster" is familiar to most people because of the many news bulletins that are issued when sightings are reported. While not considered to be a real living creature by many, the number of sightings indicates that something resembling a plesiosaur pays frequent visits to the lake. With the development of sonar, Loch Ness has been used as a test area for new sonar devices. The murky water does not allow direct visibility into its depths, and known landmarks in the lake provide the targets for sonar detection. One such target is a sunken barge. Figure 46 is a reproduction of a sonar scan showing the sunken barge along with an underwater creature that is about the same length as the barge. (Snigier, Paul, 1976) The creature has the general size and shape of a plesiosaur. The elongate object on the left side of the plesiosaur and parallel to it is best explained as a young plesiosaur being escorted by the adult.

Another plesiosaur-type creature that gained international attention was that of a rotting corpse hauled in by a Japanese fishing vessel off the coast of New Zealand in 1977. The Japanese took samples of flesh from the creature before returning it to the sea. Analysis of the samples showed it to be from the plesiosaurus family. Shortly after the publicity of this strange catch reached modern evolutionary scientists, disclaimers were issued calling it a decaying shark. But the photographs taken by the Japanese and their physical analysis of the tissue samples do not support the accusations of the disclaimers.

Malcolm Bowden reviewed the Japanese papers (Sasaki, T., 1978.) and other published articles written from both those supporting the plesiosaurus identification and those in opposition. "A careful reading of the CPC report leads me to the conclusion that it was specifically geared to dismissing the possibility that the carcass was a plesiosaur-type animal." (Bowden, Malcolm, no date) Bowden shows in detail why the remains are that of a mammal and not of a fish.

One event related to men and dinosaurs that influenced art and literature like no other is related to St. George and the dragon. Art galleries from a variety of nations show the artistic interpretations of St. George spearing a dragon. Statues have been erected to honor the event. The man-eating creature that is described in words often takes on rather small dimensions by comparison to St. George in some of the artistic renditions. Figure C-68 is a more realistic interpretation.

EVIDENCE FOR RAPID SEDIMENTATION AND FOSSILIZATION

A fossilized baby dinosaur "hatchling" was found in a ravine near Decatur, Texas. It had evidently been eroded out of the limestone layers that formed the walls of the ravine. This fossil indicates that the baby dinosaur had become buried in limestone mud shortly after or during the process of hatching since pieces of the shell were attached to the fossil. See Figure C-69. As the mud hardened into limestone the form of the dinosaur was preserved. After the flesh decayed, it was replaced by minerals percolating through the limestone. The original bones were preserved as shown in the C scan, Figure 47, that was made at Harris Hospital, Fort Worth, Texas on March 22, 1995.

In 1912, a small iron pot, apparently used for melting lead or other metals with a low temperature melting point, was found inside a large piece of coal that came from the Wilburton, Oklahoma Mines. Frank J. Kinnard, an employee of the Thomas, Oklahoma municipal electric plant, broke the piece of coal with a sledgehammer. The iron pot fell out, leaving its impression in the coal. Another employee, Jim Stull, witnessed the event. A notarized affidavit, written by Mr. Kinnard, is dated Nov. 27, 1948.

Masses of vegetation, held in suspension by the catastrophic waters of the Flood, settled out of the water between layers of sediment

Figure C-68

Typical artistic depiction of St. George and the
Dragon

Fig. 3—This trace, one of many, shows a submerged barge (a) appearing as an
X-shape, and an inexplicable form **(b)** next to it that had not appeared on the trace in
previous investigations.

Figure 46   Sonar Scan

EDN NOVEMBER 5, 1976

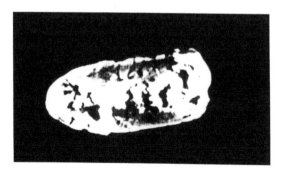

Figure 47 Scan of Dinosaur Hatching

and eventually turned into coal. The iron pot, caught up in the waters, became trapped in vegetation and remained there until the blow from the sledgehammer released it. Coal, dated by conventional geology as being millions of years old, containing a human artifact supports both the Biblical young earth and the flood of Noah as stated in our philosophical position.

Figure C-70 shows, for size comparison, a human hand holding the pot that now resides at the Creation Evidence Museum in Glen Rose, Texas.

Modern dinosaur sightings

Dinosaurs in the Lake Tele region of the Congo have been reported infrequently for more than 400 years. Pygmies, living in the rain forest area around Lake Tele, have identified the types of dinosaurs when shown pictures of different species. The Apatosaurus type is often identified. The native name for this creature is mokele mbembe.

Two other types identified are the Triceratops (emela ntouka) and the Stegosaurus (mbeilu mbeilu mbeilu).

South East Asia is another location where evidence of recent dinosaur existence is reported.

Pterodactyl sightings in New Guinea have been reported since the days of WW II when military personnel saw some. These large creatures are known to be nocturnal but on occasion are seen in the daytime. The native name for them is Ropen.

In 1994, Creation Evidence Museum sponsored an expedition to Papau New Guinea for the purpose of investigating reports on the sightings of Ropen and hopefully to see and photograph one.

Interviews with eyewitnesses or persons who knew eyewitnesses provided the following information:

A teacher from a Lutheran school stated that periodically, about once a month for a number of months, Ropen would land on his roof at night, making the whole house shake when it landed. He could hear it walking around, and was afraid during the time it was there.

Another teacher from the Lutheran school stated that some men she knew found Ropen supposedly asleep near the ocean shore. They tied a rope around its feet and tied the other end to a driftwood log. The big bird awoke and flew away with the log.

At another location, an old man related that when an old lady from the village died and was being buried at a graveyard near a river bluff, Ropen came and sat in a tree waiting for the people to leave. The people were suspicious of Ropen and stayed around for a while. But after they left, Ropen came down from the tree, dug through the river bluff into the grave and took the body.

The native people considered Ropen to a symbol of evil and sometimes called it a snake. Most were reluctant to talk about it for fear of some evil happening to them. There were reports of seeing Ropen flying at night by observing its lights, which it could turn on and off.

The expedition team did not see any Ropen.
Ref. Transcript of the notebook kept by M. E. Clark, 1994

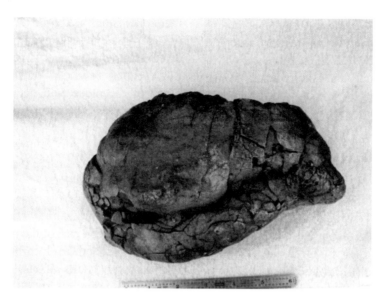

Figure C-69
Dinosaur hatchling, Texas – Cretaceous
fossil

Figure C-70
Iron pot from coal, Oklahoma

CONCLUSIONS

Prior to 1984, the scientific evidence for the coexistence of men and dinosaurs seemed to be quite convincing for those who accepted the Biblical view of a recent creation in which both animals and man began to live in harmony in a perfect world. The subsequent fall into sin and the increasing wickedness of man resulted in a Divine judgment, the flood of Noah. We believe this was the event that produced the evidence of coexistence now contained in the Cretaceous limestone beds along the Paluxy River near Glen Rose, Texas. Human-like tracks were reported being found in the early 1900's along with many dinosaur tracks. In 1969 Stan Taylor began gathering information for the film Footprints in Stone, and additional evidence was produced which countered the claim that the human-like tracks had been carved. Creationists, most of whom had not seen the evidence first hand, now had scientific support for their belief in coexistence. The evidence was only circumstantial since no human remains had been found in the area.

In the early 1980s, investigators of the Paluxy tracks began documenting characteristics of the Taylor trail that were definitely dinosaurian in nature. When the Paluxy River bed was nearly dry in 1984, detailed information about the Taylor trail was disclosed that altered the earlier assessment of the trail.

A controversy arose over what had originally been discovered, and earlier documentation was reviewed. The formation of the special task force by the Bible-Science Association brought us into the investigation activities that are now documented in this report.

In the Introduction, an emphasis was made as to the importance of presuppositions in arriving at conclusions. Our stated presuppositions of a young earth, a universal flood, rapid fossilization, changed environment and limitations in carbon 14 dating are part of the context within which gathered evidences have been evaluated.

Our conclusions are based on re-examination of older evidence and examination of newly discovered evidence. Time has taken its toll (second law of thermodynamics) on much of the older evidence because of the steady erosion processes of the river and the environment. Erosion processes have contributed to the controversy because details previously unseen or not understood were revealed or enhanced as the rock layers in the river were worn down. Infilling of tracks and identification thereof by color contrast has been part of the new information that has resulted in locating more tracks and defining details of earlier tracks. The suspected altering of tracks by staining was shown to be only suspicion. Upon reaching that conclusion we then started on the task of gathering new information.

Taylor Trail

Of particular importance is the information obtained from reexamination of the Taylor trail since it was the focal point of the film Footprints in Stone and the center of the controversy. There was a limited amount of detailed documentation from the original Taylor trail investigation to adequately support the early claims of human-like foot characteristics such as toes and heel depressions. When the color outlines of dinosaur features became evident, some were quick to suspect tampering.

Conclusions reached from examination of 1984 photographs, portions of the film Footprints in Stone and Stan Taylor's 1969 notes were that dinosaur track features existed to some extent from the time the trail was exposed. It was in 1988, when the river again was nearly dry, that Patton and Baugh documented each of the tracks in the Taylor trail with photographs and casts. Even though there had been more erosion, there was also more color definition of the dinosaur track.

Secondary impressions in the dinosaur tracks were in various parts of the track outline showing that they were not a characteristic of the dinosaur foot. Detractors who have said that there is no evidence for human-like tracks have not adequately explained the variation in location of these secondary impressions and their consistent length.

Comparison of the 1969 +1 track outline with the 1988 +1 eroded outline shows a definite correlation. Track -3B, in 1988, revealed clear human-like toe impressions when the track was thoroughly cleaned. A left-right pattern was observed in the trail sequence. This was further verified by the double-blind test performed with college students at Wichita State University by Professor Paul Ackerman. Examination of part of the trail in 1992 revealed another important feature that the +6 track of distinct human-like characteristics was outside the adjacent dinosaur track that had previously been unobserved. Evaluation of this track from 3D slides taken in 1992 also shows another 5-inch human-like track superimposed on the 11-inch human-like track.

This amount of evidence leads to the conclusion that the Taylor trail is a sequence of superimposed human-like footprints over tridactyl dinosaur prints up to the last identifiable prints in the trail where the two tracks are side-by-side. This overprinting explains track contours that do not fit a normal dinosaur foot impression.

Clark Trail
New evidence to support earlier findings is found in the Clark trail which consists of 5 tracks (some partial) in sequence plus another track of the same dimensions and in the same limestone layer in a nearby location. The clearest of the Clark series, track +3C, was examined by the Dallas Crime Lab Forensic Department and declared to be a human footprint.

Two tracks of the Clark series are partial because one was by the fossil lepidodendron that was evidently stepped on, and the other was partially obliterated by a dinosaur track. Two trails of dinosaur tracks are in close proximity to the 5-track sequence. There is anticipation that more of this trail can be exposed since it appears to parallel the river, but as of late 1993 no further tracks have been found.

On the basis of existing evidence this sequence of tracks appears to be of human-like origin.

Tracks and Trails from Continuing Investigation

Additional details on the Taylor Trail were obtained from reviewing 3D slides of the trail. These details add support to the overprinting assessment of the trail. A significant observation in the +5 track human-like overprint is a lateral depression that matches the foot pattern of a human foot. The lateral depression could not be from the dinosaur foot depression.

The Coffee track, taken from an area distant from the Paluxy River, is another example of an adult track in proximity to a child track. Lack of documentation of the series of tracks from which this track came limits the scientific impact, but the track analysis shows the track to be genuine and not a carving.

The fossil handprint found north of the Glen Rose area is another "fortunate" discovery and recovery. It indicates that human activity was not limited to a small region during the catastrophic events that produced the extensive limestone layers.

Continuing excavation and exploration of the Paluxy riverbed has resulted in extending earlier trails of both dinosaur and human-like tracks. Some individual tracks have been found where trail extension is limited by overburden or termination of rock ledges.

The general conclusion that man, dinosaurs and many other creatures were leaving their tracks in rapidly hardening mud is further supported by tracks located outside of Texas in Oklahoma, New Mexico, Arizona and even in the Eastern European country of Turkmenistan.

Fossil Teeth

The three fossil teeth that have been found to date have not been proven to be human although the general morphology matches that of human teeth. Dentists have no problem identifying them as being indicative of human incisors. They have identifiable human characteristics except for the enamel microstructure that is in the category of being inconclusive since no matching patterns have been found in an identified species. Although some have claimed them to be fish incisors, the root structure does not match a known fish. A fish incisor is mounted on a pedicle and has no root. The three fossil teeth have partial roots that appear to be broken off. As stated in the analysis section of the report, there are certain similarities to fish teeth and there are distinct differences.

We must wait for more definitive evidence before making a positive identification.

Fossil Finger

The fossil finger, while not a recent find, has identifiable internal structure like a normal human finger. It also has the finger nail outline preserved so that one does not have to guess at the similarity to a human finger. The limestone beds where this fossil was found, although several miles from the river, are of the same general system as that in the river valley.

It is unfortunate that more of the "body" was not discovered. But this is the type of evidence that gives us hope that sooner or later a fossilized human body will be found, not that it will convince the skeptics. People will not be convinced against their will.

Burdick Track

Additional sectioning of the Burdick track has revealed unmistakable pressure patterns that support its authenticity. The rock layer from which it originated has been identified by the unique characteristics of this layer and confirmed by thin-section analysis. It was found in the area described by persons who knew of its origin.

Physical characteristics of the Burdick track have been compared with similar characteristics from other fossil tracks. Tracks of similar size, while showing variation, indicate that the Burdick track fits in the range of known human tracks.

Hammer

This artifact, although found some miles from the Glen Rose area, is from Cretaceous deposits and testifies to intelligent design to which modern craftsmen can relate. The superb quality of the metal, as determined by the tomographic analysis, shows technological accomplishment that rivals or exceeds that of modern industry. This fits our understanding of the capabilities of early man who was created with intelligence. From Scripture (Genesis 4:22) we have the record that pre-flood men were skilled in working with iron and brass.

The probability of finding another artifact in the Cretaceous deposits is considered to be extremely remote for several reasons. First, by the time in the flood catastrophe that these deposits were being laid down, there were probably very few human survivors. Second, those who were still surviving would not likely have retained many artifacts. Third, the vast area over which the survivors appear to have been roaming and the limited amount of exposed sedimentary layers that can be examined further reduces the probability of finding any artifact that might be there.

Hammer Reexamined

The retest of the hammer composition showed some differences from the Battelle Labs measurements done some years ago. Initial interpretation of the Battelle composition of iron, chlorine and sulfur was that these elements were alloyed. Results of the retest show that this interpretation was false. Chlorine and sulfur were corrosion elements found near the surface of the hammer. Variations in the retest results are attributable to the varying amounts of surface corrosion. Since much of the corrosion was produced during wet conditions in the rock encasing the hammer, and the corrosion is found in thin layers, this is an indication of aging. The hammer is not a recently lost miner's tool.

Lepidodendron

Finding the fossil lepidodendron in Cretaceous limestone does not directly support our basic objective, but because it is polystrate, it does show fast deposition of the sedimentary layers. It further demonstrates that the philosophical basis for the geological column is in question since this plant type supposedly existed some 150 million or more years before the Cretaceous period. Out-of-place fossil evidences are often ignored by secular scholars. For creationists they are substantiating evidence for a global catastrophe.

Artifacts

Footprints of men and dinosaurs in the same rock stratum are significant evidence for their coexistence. The varied artifacts left by eyewitnesses of living dinosaurs in the not-too-distant past portray vivid pictures of interaction between man and dinosaurs as well as specific details of the creatures. Ancient artworks show physical details only recently determined from studying fossils. Some of the figurines found near Acambaro, Mexico are caricatures with exaggerated features. The artists who made them are no different from modern sculptors, painters or cartoonists who often resort to using caricatures of animals or people.

Historical records of dragons, sea monsters and flying reptiles add to the list of evidence for coexistence of men and dinosaurs.

In Scriptural Context

This collection of information may be circumstantial as far as proving the coexistence of men and dinosaurs scientifically, but all of it has been shown to be genuine except for a positive verification of the origin of the fossil teeth. Months of detailed analysis of the evidence have verified what we believed to be true, consistent with our presuppositions. The evidence fits the Bible's historical record of a world-wide catastrophic flood that was God's judgment on a wicked and evil world according to Genesis 6:5. God's decision to destroy man from the face of the earth as stated in Genesis 6:7 appears to have been quite successful since there is so little evidence of pre-flood man.

Consider the conditions that prevailed at the time the tracks were being made in the Glen Rose limestone beds. There was more than 150,000 square miles of limestone mud with no growing plants for plant eating reptiles that are roaming around searching for food and trying to survive. They may have been seeking refuge in the Llano uplift area since most tracks seem to center around that geological location, but, as catastrophic conditions continued or even worsened, they began roaming farther away looking for food and refuge. The question has been raised as to why men were in the vicinity of an apparently large group of dinosaurs. In a non-tranquil, survival situation, the natural survival instincts would tend to prevail, whether rational or not. Men may have been following a group of dinosaurs that could spot forage from farther away because of their height.

What is most amazing about the evidence in

the Cretaceous limestone is that there were a few who survived up to the time the Glen Rose and subsequent layers were laid down. Beneath these layers are thousands of feet of primarily sedimentary Flood deposits that cover the basement rock of the continent. From our understanding of Scripture, we know that those whose tracks we find, both animals and apparently man, soon would have succumbed to the catastrophe.

We have previously stated that much has been learned from the continued examination of the fossil evidences found in and around the Glen Rose area. More will undoubtedly be found to add to the database supporting our conclusions of coexistence of men and dinosaurs.

Note: For a biblical description of dinosaurs, see Job 40:15 ff for a land-dwelling type, and Job 41:1 ff for a sea-dwelling type.

Recommendations

The authors would like to leave several recommendations. First, keep the up-to-date information relating to the coexistence of men and dinosaurs available to the public using the Internet, seminars, Creation Science meetings and other opportunities.

Second, in order to remove the uncertainty about the origin of the fossil teeth because of the lack of complete human fossil evidence with which to make a comparison, there needs to be a repeat of the radio-immuno assay test conducted with a quality sample. It is recognized that there are significant expenses involved, but there is significant merit to be gained. Whatever the results, it will add to our knowledge of these fossils.

Third, don't stop digging. The educational benefits to the many students and other volunteers who become involved are immeasurable. And who knows what might turn up under the next rock section.

REFERENCES

Aitken, M. J., 1998. An Introduction to Optical Dating. Oxford University Press, Oxford

Baugh, Carl E. with Wilson, Clifford A., *Dinosaur*, 1987

Beierle, Fredrick, A New Kind of Evidence from the Paluxy, *Creation Research Society Quarterly*, Sept. 1979; Radiocarbon dating: *UCLA-2088*, 10-23-78

Beierle, Fredrick, *Man, Dinosaur and History*, 1980

Bowden, Malcolm, THE JAPANESE CARCASS: A PLESIOSAUR-TYPE MAMMAL! A review of the evidence, page 12, Creation Science Movement, Portsmouth, England.

Cavanagh, P. R., Kram, R., 1989. Stride length in distance running: velocity, body dimensions and added mass effects. Med. Sci. Sports Exerc. 21, 467-479.

Cooper, Bill, *After the Flood*, **The early post-flood history of Europe traced back to Noah**, New Wine Press, 1995

Films For Christ Association, Footprints in Stone: The Current Situation, *Origins Research* Vol. 9 No. 1 1986

Garbe, R, H. Miller, J. Whitmore, G. Detwiler, D. Wilder, F. Vosler, J. Ditmars, D. Davis, **Direct Dating of Cretaceous-Jurassic Fossils**, *Proceedings of the 1992 Twin-Cities Creation Conference*, August 1992, pp 7-13

Hastings R. J. Mantracks Again?--Not Really (2-1-89) received by mail from Dr. Hastings

Hastings, Ron J. The Rise and Fall of the Paluxy Man Tracks, *Perspectives on Science and the Christian Faith*, Vol. 40 No.3, Sept 1988

Huntley, D. J., Godfrey-Smith, D. I., Thewalt, M. L. W., 1985, Optical dating of sediments, *Nature* 313, 105-107.

Koenig, Earl, **Roman Relics Found in Arizona**, *Ancient American*, Vol. 5, Issue 36, Dec. 2000
[Eppinga, Jane, "If They Were Aspirin: Questions About the Tucson Artifacts", **The Epigraphic Society Occasional Papers**, Vol. 19 (no date)]

Kuban, Glen J., Color Distinction and Other Curious Features of Dinosaur Tracks Near Glen Rose, Texas, Presented at *First International Symposium on Dinosaur Tracks and Traces*, Albuquerque, New Mexico, May 1986

Laskowski and Kyle, "Barefoot Impressions--A Preliminary Study of Identification Characteristics and Population Frequency of Their Morphological Features", *Journal of Forensic Sciences* Vol. 3, No. 2, March 1988

McGlenn, Russell, **Mystery of the Effigy Mounds**, Adventure Safaris, 1996)

Menton, Dr. David, Letter to Paul Bartz, dated November 18,1987.

Morris, John D. "Continued Research on the Paluxy Tracks" *Acts and Facts*, Vol. 17 No 12, December 1988

Morris, John D., Letter to Robert F. Helfinstine dated June 27, 1986; *SOR Bulletin* Vol. 2 No.4 Dec. 1986

Morris, John D., Letter to Robert F. Helfinstine dated Sept 22, 1986; also Identification of Ichnofossils in the Glen Rose Limestone, Central Texas, paper presented at Duquesne

University, Pittsburgh, August 1986; *SOR Bulletin* Vol. 2 No. 4 Dec. 1986

Morris, John, *Tracking Those Incredible Dinosaurs & the People Who Knew Them*, Master Books, 1980

Origins Research Vol. 8 No. 2 Fall/Winter 1985

Parker, Gary and Morris, Henry, *What is Creation Science* P.126, 1982

Patton, Don R., Lecture at *1992 Twin-Cities Creation Conference*, July 29-Aug. 1, 1992

Peterson, Dale H. MD, letter to Dennis Petersen, March 27, 2002

Peyer, B., *Comparative Odontology* (Univ. of Chicago Press, 1968, p. 16, Statement about opposing incisors occurring in mammals, as quoted by Baugh, Carl, in *Creation Evidences from the Paluxy*, Vol. 3 No.1.

Rosnau, Auldaney, Howe and Waisgerber, Are Human And Mammal Tracks Found Together With the Tracks of Dinosaurs in the Kayenta of Arizona?; Part II A Field Study of Quasihuman, Quasimammalian, and Dinosaur Ichnofossils Near Tuba City, *CRS Quarterly*, Dec. 1989

Sasaki, T. editor, CPC –Collected Papers on the Carcass of an Unidentified Animal Trawled off New Zealand by the Zuiyo-maru, 1978, La Societe Franco-Japonaise d'Oceanographie, Tokyo

Science News Online, Jan. 7, 2006, Vol. 169, No. 1, (**Stone Age Footwork: Ancient human prints turn up down under**, Bruce Bower)

Snigier, Paul, **Three-channel side-scan sonar detects Loch Ness "monster" and ancient ruins**, **EDN** Technical magazine, Nov. 5, 1976

Somervell Sun Vol. 1 No. 47, Wed. June 24, 1987

Stolk, Douglas A., Metallurgical Engineering Services, Inc. **Composition and Morphology Analysis**, July 14, 2002

Swift, Dennis, *Secrets of the Ica Stones and Nazca Lines*, 2006, p. 136

Ten Cate, A. R., Oral Histology: Development, Structure and Function

The 1992 Twin-Cities Creation Conference, July 29 to Aug. 1, 1992, Northwestern College, St. Paul, MN

Tuttle, Russell H., "The Pitted Pattern of Laetoli Feet", *Natural History*, 3/90.

Watson, John Allen, **Man, Dinosaurs and Mammals Together**, Mt. Blanco Publishing Co., 2001

Webb, S., M. L. Cupper and R. Robins, Pleistocene human footprints from the Willandra Lakes, southeastern Australia, *Journal of Human Evolution*, April 2006, pp 405-413

Woelfel, Julian B., *Dental Anatomy*, 3rd Edition, 1984

Woodmorappe, John, A Diluvio-logical Treatise on the Stratigraphical Separation of Fossils, II E Cause for the (Near) Absence of Pre-Pleistocene Human Fossils, *CRS Quarterly*, Vol. 20, Dec 1983, P 171

A WORD ON FOSSILS

Fossils are prior life forms that have been unusually preserved in a variety of ways. The following are the types identified in **Earth Story**, A science textbook produced by the Seventh-day Adventist Department of Education.

Type #1 <u>Impressions</u>: These include shell, bone, footprints, etc. Most common are tracks (ichnofossils) in mud or sand turned into rock (e.g. dinosaur, animal, human).

Type #2 <u>Petrified fossils</u>: These are formed when mineral transported by water replaces the organic material cell by cell as decay takes place (e.g. petrified wood, animals, jellyfish, dinosaur skin, shells).

Type #3 <u>Carbonization</u>: Living or organic matter leaves a carbon film outline of the specimen (e.g. leaf, fish, delicate organism). The best example of carbonization is vegetation turned to coal.

Type #4 <u>Unchanged fossils</u>: Bones have been preserved in tar pits such as the La Brea tar pits in southern California. A complete human fossil was found in a peat bog in Denmark. Siberia and Alaska have frozen animals, bones and vegetation in the permafrost. Amber fossils are formed when tree sap captures a life form like an insect, and the sap becomes petrified. Shell material, teeth, bones and wood have been preserved in sedimentary strata.

Note: Hard parts like shells, bone or teeth are the most likely to be fossilized as this material does not decay quickly. Most fossils are preserved in sedimentary rock (water laid) where the mud has hardened primarily due to mineral cementing and pressure.

INDIRECT EVIDENCE OF PLANTS and ANIMALS
(Original decayed away)

<u>Molds</u>: Fossil evidences such as clams and snails are often found as molds. These can be seen as portions of or as complete animal impressions in rock where the organisms have completely decayed away. The mold forms a three dimensional outline of what the living form looked like. These can be either inside molds or outside molds.

<u>Cast</u>: If an outside mold fills in with another water-transported mineral, the infill material forms a cast of the original organism. In practice the infilled material can be identified as an internal mold if it is separated from the original outside mold.

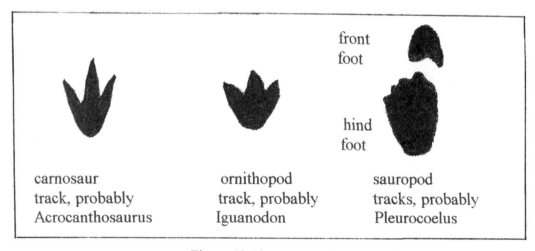

carnosaur track, probably Acrocanthosaurus

ornithopod track, probably Iguanodon

front foot

hind foot

sauropod tracks, probably Pleurocoelus

Figure 48 Dinosaur Tracks

Discussion: The major factor in preservation of fossils is that the animal or vegetation must be buried quickly and deep enough to keep out free oxygen. If oxygen is present, bacteria or fungi can cause decay to occur too rapidly for preservation to take place. The many clam fossils in the Glen Rose limestone where tracks are also found were most likely buried alive, as the shell halves are not separated. When a clam or other pelecypod dies its shell halves open up in a short time due to muscle relaxation. Half shells are commonly found along ocean, lake and river shores. Tracks and ripple marks must also be buried quickly in order to preserve them.

GEOLOGY CONSIDERATIONS

Geology deals with the history of the earth, particularly as that history is recorded in the rocks. Interpretation of the rock formations depends on the presuppositions of the interpreter. Based on a "young earth" creation model and a subsequent universal flood, evidences found in the rock formations are easily understood from a Flood Geology perspective.

DATING OF ROCKS AND FOSSILS

Dating Techniques

The age of the earth is considered by many to be 4.5 billion years. This number appears in most science textbooks, often without information as to how it was derived. Dating techniques for geological formations has been changing over the past several hundred years as new techniques are developed. It was the discovery of radiometric dating and its application to earth crystalline rock that resulted in a large increase in the assumed age of the earth.

Earlier dating was accomplished by such processes as measuring the accumulation of minerals and salts in the ocean, counting the annual deposits in the deltas at mouths of rivers, measuring erosion of waterfalls, measuring accumulation of meteorite dust or measuring the decay of the earth's magnetic field. Most dates derived from these processes were in the range from several thousand years to several hundred million years. In all such processes the accuracy of the result depends heavily on the assumptions used. The same is true in the calculation of the 4.5 billion year date, but most persons are unaware of those assumptions.

Not all rocks are dated by the same methods. Radiometric dating is not directly used to determine the age of sedimentary rocks. The geological column and the assumed ages of fossil bearing strata were derived before radiometric dating was developed. Sedimentary strata are not dated by their vertical sequence, their mineral content or their physical characteristics. They are primarily dated by fossil content, but not total fossil content. Certain fossils are known as index fossils such as trilobites and dinosaurs. These have been assigned to certain time periods based on evolutionary theory. If trilobites and dinosaurs are found in the same strata, the trilobites would be ignored (because they are not supposed to be there) and the rock layer will be called Cretaceous to fit the assigned nomenclature of the geologic column. Mixing or reworking of material may be given as the reason for anomalous fossil conditions.

Radiometric dating techniques are used on crystalline rocks such as granites, basalt and quartz. Small amounts of radioactive material are found distributed within the rock. Radioactive decay is a natural process by which an unstable Parent isotope* decays, through a series of steps or a single step, depending on the Parent element, to a stable Daughter isotope. Measuring the amounts of the Parent isotope and the Daughter isotope and knowing the decay rate can, by proper calculations, provide a "radiometric date" for a rock sample. This may or may not be the true age of the rock. The assumptions are key in arriving at radiometric dates, but the assumptions are not proven and are not provable.

The main assumptions of the predominant testing methods in the uranium-lead or rubidium-strontium series are:

1. The rock system must be closed. There must have been no gain or loss of either Parent or Daughter isotope during the life of the rock.
2. There was no initial Daughter isotope.
3. The decay process is known and is constant.
4. The measurement of the Parent and Daughter isotopes is accurate.

There are several problems with these assumptions. It is doubtful that there are completely closed systems over long periods of time, it is impossible to know the initial conditions or whether or not the decay process has changed, and measurement accuracies may depend on the skills of the operators.

Additional factors limit the ability to determine accurate dates. Mixing of molten magma with surrounding rock can cause exchange of both parent and daughter material that will alter the measured ratios. And the parent/daughter ratio may not have been homogenous in the molten material when it was cooling into hard rock.

Dating of organic fossils, such as once living plant or animal remains, is usually done by the radiocarbon (^{14}C) method. Since the decay rate of ^{14}C is much faster than that of the minerals used to date rocks, it has an upper time limit that some claim to be 50,000 or more years. Most would accept limits of about 15,000 years for reasonable accuracy. As with the other radiometric dating techniques, knowing the assumptions is important in understanding the accuracy of the results.

Assumptions for radiocarbon dating are:
1. The generation activity for ^{14}C is a known constant.
2. It is independent of time for 70,000 years.
3. The value is independent of geographical location.
4. The percentage of ^{14}C is not species dependent.
5. There is no ^{14}C contamination.
6. There is no loss of ^{14}C except by radioactive decay.
7. The decay rate is known and constant.

Some of the assumptions listed have known limitation. Because of the shorter half-life of ^{14}C, its decay rate can be determined more accurately than that of uranium, but it cannot be proven that the rate has not changed. There are known changes in the generation rate due to sun activity and changes in the earth's magnetic field. Also there are known losses of ^{14}C due to physical and chemical actions in nature. The older a specimen is, the less is the accuracy of its age determination because the amount of radiocarbon is continually decreasing. After 8 half lives, the remaining ^{14}C is less than .4% of the original amount. Therefore, the sample is subject to influence from adjacent material. There is also evidence that it is species dependent and sometimes sensitive to geographic location. Different types of materials of the same known age have been 14C dated with results showing significantly different "radiometric ages".

* An isotope is one of two or more elements identical in chemical behavior but having small differences in atomic weight.

Formation of Continental Granite Basement Rock

It is generally assumed that the large 20,000 foot granite structures, which underlie the continents, were formed gradually during cooling of the global mass. The transformation from a liquid to a solid state presumably took millions of years. True granite has never been produced from a melt in controlled laboratory conditions.

In the crystalline structure of the granite there are radioactive inclusions as indicated in the section on **Dating Techniques**. During the decay of the radioactive isotopes, the emission of alpha particles causes damage to the crystalline structure of the rock. Isotopes of different elements in the decay chain lose alpha particles having different energy levels. The damage pattern from alpha emissions is in the form of small concentric spheres called Pleochroic halos surrounding the parent radioactive inclusion. Each sphere can be associated with a particular isotope in the inclusion. When a sphere is cut in half for viewing under a microscope, it is viewed as concentric circles. In the uranium/lead decay series there are several isotopes of polonium (Po), very unstable radioactive elements with short half lives. The half-life of ^{218}Po is 3.05 minutes, the half-life of ^{214}Po is 1.5 microseconds, and ^{210}Po has a half-life of 138 days.

The halos caused by polonium decay are usually associated with the parent uranium halos. However there are numerous halos consisting only of those from polonium with none from the parent uranium. The only rational conclusion that can be given for these halos to exist is that the granite was formed "instantaneously" as hard rock with polonium inclusions that rapidly decayed, leaving their unique signature. If the rock matrix had been molten, the polonium would have decayed without leaving a trace of its existence. The only proposed alternative explanation for the polonium halos is the assumption that uranium moved through the granite, leaving the polonium halos where it stopped. Advanced technical analysis has disproved this explanation since no traces of uranium or alpha recoil particle damage sufficient for verification of uranium

movement was located in the vicinity of the polonium halos. It would be difficult for uranium to move through granite, as the alternate explanation requires. It would also violate one of the major assumptions for radiometric dating, that granite or other rocks are closed systems.

This evidence supports the Bible's description of the creation of the heavens and earth by the word of God.

Radiometric Dating of Coalified Wood

Coal and coalified wood are assumed to be too old to be dated by ^{14}C methods. However, there are known samples of coal that have been dated by this method with results showing wide ranges of radiometric ages.

In recent years R. V. Gentry has taken coalified wood from the Colorado Plateau and used the uranium/lead dating technique to arrive at the radiometric age. This was possible because during the coalification process when the buried trees were in a water-soaked gel-like state they were infiltrated with a uranium solution. Some uranium particles became trapped. The uranium/lead ratios in the inclusions were measured, and the radiometric dates were calculated to be in the 5,000 year time frame rather than the 60 million to 200 million year time frame assigned to samples from Triassic, Jurassic and Eocene deposits. The measured age of the coalified wood appears consistent with the Biblical history of the earth and particularly the world wide flood of Noah which was evidently responsible for depositing the wood from the different formations in a relatively short time.

Because of the unique situation that deposited the uranium in the wood, Gentry looked for secondary polonium and found many samples. They were all of ^{210}Po that has a half-life of 138 days. After separating from the parent uranium inclusion, the polonium became trapped and lived long enough to form its characteristic halo, probably less than one year. But most of the halos were elliptical rather than circular in cross section. The original circular patterns had been compressed by the increasing weight of the overburden.[1] Their occurrence in the three identified geological formations is another indication that there was a common event responsible for the coal deposits, the flood of Noah.

A few dual halos were found in the coalified wood, one elliptical and the other circular, formed around the same inclusion. The first was formed by 210Po as stated above. The second was initiated by ^{210}Pb (lead) with a half-life of 22 years that decays into ^{210}Po. The subsequent ^{210}Po decay after the wood was compressed produced the circular halos.

1. **Breger, I. A**. 1974. "Formation of Uranium Ore Deposits" *Proceedings of a Symposium*, Athens, May 6-10, Vienna: International Atomic Energy Agency

See *Creation's Tiny Mystery*, by Robert V. Gentry for detail information.

Mount St. Helens

We have at Mount St. Helens a real time demonstration of fast erosion and sedimentation. The events which occurred over a period of little more than a decade show that long ages are not needed to produce large scale geological changes and that recovery to a "near normal" state occurs quite rapidly.

Erosion:
The major blast occurred on May 18, 1980 with much destruction and erosion caused by earthquakes, shock waves, water and mud runoff from melting snow and thawing of frozen ground, and volcanic ash. On March 19,1982, 22 months after the initial blast, a moderate explosion caused a snow melt which sent a mud flow down the north fork of the Toutle River. This flow quickly formed a miniature Grand Canyon 100 feet deep, cutting through layers of stratified sediment that had been deposited on June 12, 1980. Erosion of this magnitude is usually attributed to slow changes by small streams over a long period of time by orthodox geology. This documented demonstration of fast erosion fits in with other history. Some ancient Indian records identify a period of catastrophic conditions that caused many of the canyons of the western United States to be formed.

Rapid Sedimentation
Up to 600 feet of sedimentary strata were formed around Mount St. Helens since 1980 including some ground hugging flow deposits. The stratified sediments deposited on June 12, 1980 consisted of thin layers (laminae) and cross-bedding (inclined to the horizontal), features that are usually attributed to long slow processes. Here they took less than one day to be formed. Water was involved and fast deposition, not the slow wind-blown process that is sometimes assumed for producing cross bedding.

Many trees were buried around and under the present Spirit Lake in this major event. The 295-foot deposit of avalanche debris and trees in Spirit Lake can be compared to Amethyst Ridge in Yellowstone Park where a similar mixture of material has turned into rock, and the trees are petrified.

A large quantity of trees ended up in a floating mat on Spirit Lake. Some of the floating trees have made a gradual transition to a vertical root-down position, and many have subsequently settled to the bottom where they are being slowly covered with sediment. The resulting stepped arrangement of buried vertical trees can be correlated with trees buried in a mountain exposure of Yellowstone Park that are explained as the gradual burial of a series of growing forests over many thousands of years. The Mount Saint Helens burial process has been going on for less than 30 years.

Potential for Coal Formation

Coal is formed from buried vegetation, but the process by which it is formed has several proposed scenarios. Dr. Steve Austin, in his doctoral dissertation in 1979, proposed a floating mat model for the formation of the #12 coal bed of western Kentucky. This coal bed has significant amounts of coalified tree bark. Dr. Austin's model was in sharp contrast to the orthodox view of peat bog or swamp models of coal formation. The floating mat model has an allochthonous (originating elsewhere) explanation for coal formation, whereas the swamp model (autochthonous) assumes an in-place formation of coal, even though there is no evidence of soil layers or tree rooting beneath coal seams.

The Mount Saint Helens eruption in 1980 provided the first major step in demonstrating the floating mat model. On the floor of Spirit Lake a large quantity of tree bark as well as some tree material has been deposited, coming from the large floating mat of trees on the lake. Although some sedimentation from ash and runoff from the mountain covers the bark deposits, what is needed to complete the coal formation process is a significant mudflow or heavy layer of volcanic material to cover the bark.

Reference information on Mount St. Helens: Austin, Steven A., 1986, **Mount St. Helens and Catastrophism,** *Proceedings of the First International Conference on Creationism,* Pittsburgh, PA, vol.1, pp.3-9.

Grand Canyon

The Grand Canyon is the largest exposure of sedimentary rock layers on earth. Thick rock layers, as much as 1000 feet thick, can be identified by contrasting color, texture and material. Water laid muds and sands were sequentially laid down in rapid succession with no evidence of time lapse for surface erosion that would have occurred during slow deposition with interruptions in the deposition process. If long periods of time were involved, we would expect erosion within layers and/or between layers.

Faulting in sedimentary strata is often caused by earthquakes. Again, if long periods of time were involved in deposition of layers, we would expect to see faulting within a layer, erosion in the fault lines, and the subsequent layer depositing sediment within the fault. This generally is not the case. When faulting does occur, it cuts through all layers from top to bottom. Assumed long ages assigned by orthodox geology are not compatible with the evidence.

The limestone rock in the Grand Canyon is much different from what is forming today, therefore, present conditions cannot explain past limestone formation. Modern limestone composition is 65% to 95% aragonite with an approximate grain size of 20 microns. Grand Canyon limestone composition is close to 100% calcite and/or dolomite with a grain size of only 4 microns.[1]

The Coconino Sandstone (near top of canyon) has previously been explained as forming from wind-blown sand. Recent studies of this formation have shown it to be water laid because of the measured cross-bedding angle that is different from wind-blown cross-bedding angles. Animal track ways in the Coconino are best interpreted as formed in wet sand as demonstrated in laboratory experiments. This is consistent with a Flood explanation of this rock formation.

Grand Canyon rock layers do not contain some of the rock formations shown in the evolutionary geological column. There is no obvious erosion to indicate that the layers could have been there. Therefore, the vast amount of time that these "missing" rock layers represent, according to orthodox geology, never took place. Examination of the north face of the canyon shows multiple alternate layering of the Mississippian and Cambrian rock layers,[2] so identified by their fossil content. This unusual sequence is not possible per evolutionary theory.

These evidences from the Grand Canyon are best interpreted by rapid formation of water laid sediments attributable to the Noahic Flood.

1. Austin, Steven A., *Grand Canyon: Monument to Catastrophe*, p 20

2. Burdick, Clifford L., *Canyon of Canyons*, p 61

Radiocarbon Dating as it Relates to Coexistence of Men and Dinosaurs

The philosophical position of secular science is that dinosaurs lived long before man appeared on the earth. Therefore the dinosaur bones that are found are too old to show any significant amount of radiocarbon (^{14}C), and any that did show would be considered contamination.

The half-life of ^{14}C is 5700 years, thus limiting the time of useful measurements to less than 10 half lives or about 50,000 years. Another unknown factor that enters the time measurement is the ^{14}C level in the early earth atmosphere at a given time.

For those that believe in millions of years for earth history, the 50,000-year limit is a problem.
For those that hold to the literal teaching of Genesis and an earth history of about 7000 years, there has been hardly enough time for the atmospheric ^{14}C to reach equilibrium. We would expect measurements on old fossils to show an age older than the actual age if we use current conditions as a basis for age calculations.

^{14}C measurement Activities

The fact that direct measurement of ^{14}C in dinosaur bones shows measurable amounts makes documentation of additional samples a significant scientific activity. Measurements place dinosaurs in thousands of radiocarbon years, not millions of theoretical years as assumed by orthodox geology.

Initial dating of fossil remains in the Paluxy River valley was done by Fred Beierle (1979). A carbonized branch, found by Wilbur fields embedded in the Cretaceous rock of the river bottom, was subjected to radiocarbon testing. Result of the measurement was 12,800 RC years. A carbonized wood specimen that had been embedded in the rock without exposure to the atmosphere was dated at >49,900 RC years using an Accelerated Mass Spectrometer (AMS). Dr. Carl Baugh had a dinosaur bone tested for radiocarbon content using the conventional method. The date was >36,600 RC years.

Additional dinosaur bone fragments from Texas to Alaska have been radiocarbon dated with measurements ranging from 9,980 to >36,500 RC years. As expected, those believing in long ages raised objections to these relatively young dates. Stafford, in 1992, proposed that contamination was the reason for the measured results. Contamination could be from modern ^{14}C, possibly from the air or from organic chemical absorption.

To test the proposed contamination theory and simultaneously confirm that the coexistence of man and dinosaurs was verifiable, the Hugh Miller team used radiocarbon dating of fossil amber as an independent measurement of fossil time. The carbon content of amber is approximately 80 percent compared to 2-5 percent in dinosaur bones. Measuring a relatively young age for amber, which is less susceptible to contamination, would rule out contamination and verify the dating of dinosaur bones. It would also show that the dates assigned to the geologic column are excessive, thus supporting the young earth model.

Amber specimens to test for contamination were from the Hanson ranch in Wyoming. They were selected at a site where a Triceratops had been excavated. The test results by AMS were >46,450 radiocarbon years compared to the age assigned by the geologic column of 65 million years.

Radiocarbon Measurement Data

Two tables of data containing information from samples being tested for radiocarbon age, location of sample origin, radiocarbon age and measurement equipment, the evolution

paradigm, and the Creation paradigm.
Table 1 lists information for dinosaur bone fragments or bone scrapings.
Table 2 lists information for wood and other carbon datable specimens.

These tabulations were produced by Hugh Miller with inputs from CRSEF and the Paleo group of Columbus, Ohio.

TABLE 1. RADIOCARBON AGES FOR FOSSIL DINOSAUR BONE FRAGMENTS OR SCRAPINGS

Specimen, lab, Year analyzed*	Location, collector, Year	RC Years, equipment**	Evolution, Paradigm, years BP	Creation Paradigm, years BP
Acrocanthosaurus, Fragments, 1986	Glen Rose TX CEM, Baugh & Parker, 1984	>36,500 Conventional	~108,000,000 very slow deposition	~5,000 very rapid deposition-flood
Same as above, 1989	ditto, Miller arranged lab	>32,000 Conventional	ditto	ditto
Acrocanthosaurus, Fragments, Overseas lab	ditto	25,750 +/- 280, AMS	ditto	ditto
Acrocanthosaurus, Surface scrapings, UN of AZ, AA-5786, 1990	ditto	23,750 +/- 270 AMS	ditto	ditto
Allosaurus, UN of AZ/A-5810 1990	Grand Junct. CO, Liberty UN. J. Hall, 1986, Hall/Miller	16,120 +/- 220(?) Conventional	140,000,000	ditto
Camarasaurus UN of AZ, A-6339, 1990, WY	Carnegie Mus. Johnson Cty, Utterback, Miller arrang.	11,750 +/- 150 Conventional	ditto ditto	ditto ditto
Camarasaurus Un of AZ A-6340, 1990	Carnegie Mus. Johnson Cty, WY, Utterback, Miller arranged	17,420 +/- 330 Conventional	ditto	ditto
Unknown dinosaur UN of AZ, A-5809	Carnegie Mus. Dinosaur Nat. Monument, UT Miller arranged	9,890 +/- 60 Conventional	ditto	ditto
Hadrosaur, Overseas, 1995	Colville River North Slope, AK by Arctic Ocean, Whitmore team; Miller/ Giertych arranged	33,000 +/- +	ditto	ditto

*If C-14 labs know the bones are from dinosaurs, they will return them "as they are too old", so labs not noted here are ones who will date unknown samples. The University of Arizona lab was very unhappy when they learned they had dated dinosaur bones; claimed they were contaminated; they definitely were not based on Leco furnace studies before dating.

** > [greater than] means the RC date so recorded is the minimum age, but could be older, including having an "infinite or unknown age". One lab suggested "older" for the Acrocanthosaurus bones fragments [didn't know they were dinosaur bones] because such specimens in that condition [fossilized] looked older from his experience with other specimens with which he was familiar [meaning their location in the now obsolete geologic column indicated very old ages]. However, under the right conditions, artifacts such as a miner hat [Australia] absorbed minerals and became completely fossilized. Stalactites and stalagmites have been found under concrete type buildings and bridges less than 100 years old so the degree of fossilization is not a measure of age. AMS units [Accelerated Mass Spectrometers] are superior to conventional C-14 equipment in determining accuracy and precision as evidenced by a comparison of the RC ages for the Acrocanthosaurus, the top four samples [note that the actual RC ages were about 10,000 RC years younger as well.]

TABLE 2: RADIOCARBON DATING OF FOSSILIZED CARBONIZED WOOD, UNFOSSILIZED WOOD AND OTHER CARBON DATABLE SPECIMENS (a). COMPARED WITH EVOLUTIONARY AND CREATION PARADIGMS AGES

Specimen, lab, Year analyzed	Location, collector, Year	RC Years, equipment	Evolution Paradigm Age, years	Creation Paradigm Age, years
P-11A, wood Mummified surface, 2004	Ellef Ringness Is., Dr. C. Felix, geologist, 1970s	>45,700, AMS	40 M (?) very slow deposition	5,350 Very rapid deposition
Ditto but a second Lab, 2001	Ditto	52,820 + 3680/-2510	ditto	5,350
P-12, 2 ft diameter tree 120 ft deep in permafrost, 2004	Wood from Prudhoe Bay, oil geologist cousin of J. Heffner 1987	43,380+/-380 AMS	cretaceous	~5,350 Very rapid deposition
P-128, wood,( ) 30 ft deep in sand w/mammoth, 2004	Fairbanks, AK Skidmore Mine & J. Taylor, ~2001	2510+/-50 Conventional	~Same as RC age	age ~Same age as RC age
P-2, wood, 30 ft deep in sand & water w/mammoth tusk 2004	Texas Gulf coast K. Vernor Co. Taylor/Baugh consultants	44,460 +13870/-4838 conventional	Pre-flood (?)	~5,000 (?)

P-3, ivory same depth w/ P-2 wood, 2004	ditto "collagen type compounds"	4,960 +/- 50 AMS	Post flood	~4,000
P-4, carbonized (a) wood in limestone, 2004	Paluxy River top cretaceous strata w/dino prints	> 49,900 AMS	108 M Very slow deposition	~5,350 Very rapid deposition
P-99 carbonized tree bark on petrified logs	Colorado ranch hillside, W. White J. Guthrie	44,200 +/-2100	>100 M	~5,350 Very rapid deposition

(a) Between 1978 and 1989 RC dating of carbonized fossil wood from Paluxy strata gave RC ages of 38,000; 39,000; 37,480+2950/-2140; 37,420+6120/-3430 for carbonized wood in clay layers; 12,800 (burnt wood), 45,000+5550/-3250 (coalified wood and reeds) using the conventional method. AMS was used on carbonized wood embedded in the rock itself, and only exposed to the atmosphere for ½ hour during break-up of rock. A Trinity River "hearth site" near Ft. Worth gave ages of >37,000 & >38,000 in 1957 and 1962 (b).

(b) "Direct Dating of Cretaceous-Jurassic Fossils", R. Garbe, H. Miller, J. Whitmore, G. Detwiler, D. Wilder, F. Vosler, J. Ditmars, D. Davis, Proceedings of Twin Cities Creation Conference, August 1992

APPENDIX 2

Human Tracks Documented
by Jonathan Gray

International explorer, archaeologist and author, Jonathan Gray has traveled the world to gather data on ancient mysteries. He has penetrated some largely unexplored areas, including parts of the Amazon headwaters. The author has also led expeditions to the bottom of the sea and to remote mountain and desert regions of the world. He lectures internationally.

For starters, human footprints are found in undisturbed strata of virtually all geological "ages".

Yes, they've been unearthed in rock layers where the so-called "earliest" life forms appear.

Here are some examples:

* Gobi Desert: A print of a ribbed sole (shoe or sandal size 9), in sandstone rock said to be "2 million years old."

* Fisher Canyon, Nevada: A shoe print with clear traces of strong thread, in a coal seam "12 million years old."

* Pershing County, Nevada: A shoe print, showing evidence of a well-cut and double-stitched leather sole, in Triassic limestone "160 to 195 million years old."
This find was authenticated by a competent geologist of the Rockefeller Foundation in New York.

The thread is smaller than any used by shoemakers today.
The discoverer took it to New York. He took it to Columbia University. He showed it to some of the leading people at the American Museum of Natural History and turned it over to them.

But you can write to the American Museum of Natural History - and they'll tell you the report is not in their files. (I wonder why?)

Anyway, here are some more finds:

* Cow Canyon, Nevada (25 miles east of Lovelock): The graceful imprint of a well-balanced human in a coal vein of the Tertiary "period."

* England: A shoe imprint with nail heads around its outer edge, in "450 million year old" limestone.

* Antelope Springs, Utah: Prints of a man wearing shoes, in which the left foot had trodden on a trilobite, a creature of "440 million years ago."
    This Utah discovery was made in the Wheeler Formation, in the House Range east of Antelope Springs, in shaley limestone rock.

Prints included one of a child's foot, with all five toes showing dimly.

On June 1, 1968, William Meister was looking for trilobite fossils. With difficulty, he was climbing a 2000 ft high rock face. He paused, and broke off a 2-inch thick lump of rock with his geology hammer. It opened like a book, revealing a trilobite in the heel of a sandal print.

A consulting geologist was called in. He found more sandal-prints and some footprints of bare-foot children.

It would seem from this evidence that mankind and trilobites co-existed.

* Laetoli, Africa: Footprints in rock "12 million years old."

* Tulsa, Oklahoma: Footprints in rock "12 million years old."

* Carson City, Nevada: Sandal prints in Pliocene "age" rock "12 million years old."

* Glen Rose, Texas: Footprints in Cretaceous rock "70 million years old."

* Mt. Victoria, Australia: Footprint in Triassic rock "200 million years old."

* St. Louis, Missouri: Footprints in Permian rock "200 million years old."

* Bera, Kentucky: Footprints in Pennsylvanian rock "200 million years old."

* Lake Windermere, England: Sandal print in Ordovician rock "400 million years old."

Okay, I don't want to bore you. Examples are almost countless.

Do you notice something wrong with these discoveries? That's right. They contradict evolutionary geology.

EVOLUTIONARY THEORY IN TROUBLE?

If human footprints in ancient rocks are genuine, then either men existed before evolution says they should, or our dating systems are in serious error.

As James Madsen, curator of Earth Science at the University of Utah, stated for the press, concerning the trilobite-with-man find:

"There's something of a problem here, since trilobites and humans are separated by millions of years" (in theory, over 200 million!).

Indeed, this intimate simultaneous occurrence of modern (sandal-shod) man with "primitive"

trilobites is a serious problem for the evolution theory.

FAKE "FOOTPRINTS", MAYBE?

Well, you ask, could these tracks be fakes? That's a fair question.

Sorry, but many of these prints were found "inside" stratified deposits, where forgery was impossible. You see, they were found only after removal of overlying rock strata.

Important: The impressions were made at a time when the rock was soft enough to receive them by pressure.

The vast majority of the impressions came to light when the rocks were being quarried.

They were found in some cases, dozens of feet below the present surface and hundreds of yards back into the quarries.

Various scientists have independently and meticulously examined these fossil human footprints. The sand grains within each track are closer together than the grains immediately outside the tracks and elsewhere on the rock due to the pressure of the person's foot.

This is a characteristic of genuine footprints.

SIDESTEPPING THE TRUTH

Writing in *Scientific American* concerning footprints in Carboniferous rock, Albert C. Ingalls states:

"If man, or even his ape ancestor, or even that ape ancestor's early Mammalian ancestor, existed as far back as in the Carboniferous Period in any shape, then the whole science of geology is so completely wrong that all the geologists will resign their jobs and take up truck driving.

"Hence for the present at least, science rejects the attractive explanation that man made these mysterious prints in the mud of the Carboniferous Period with his feet."

Yes, that's a mouthful. But would you please read it again.

There you have a frank admission that the facts are being deliberately sidestepped.

EVIDENCE OF DISASTER

To be perfectly preserved, the tracks had to be covered ALMOST INSTANTLY. They were then buried under hundreds of feet of earth.

The person who squashed the trilobite may have taken only a few more steps before a great disaster wiped him out.

Many of these tracks were preserved in rock hundreds of feet below the present surface of the ground, as though at or near the beginning of some great catastrophic, earth-shaking event that buried many forms of life all together, some marine and some non-marine.

Here is evidence of catastrophe, and also of mankind as far back as the Precambrian, ("before the first life on earth") period.

Those are footprints.

Would you like documentation for these finds?
Just go to http://www.beforeus.com/second.php and you can order your special copy.

Jonathan Gray

ABOUT The AUTHORS

Robert F. Helfinstine is a retired professional engineer in electrical engineering who worked for Honeywell Inc. for 40 years in design and development of avionics systems. These included automatic flight control systems for aircraft, spacecraft and missiles, engine controls for booster rocket engines, and inertial navigation systems for business and commercial aviation aircraft.

He had an early interest in archeology but was sidetracked into electronics during WWII when he served in the Navy as an aviation electronics technicians mate. After graduating from the University of Minnesota in 1950 his career with Honeywell began. During the Korean War he received a commission as an electronic specialist in the U. S. Naval Reserve.

During his years in development of flight control systems, considerable experience was gained in data analysis. He developed several aircraft safety systems that were patented. Two years were spent working in the European countries of Germany and Sweden. It was while working in Sweden that a renewed interest in archeology eventually led to his getting involved with the Twin Cities Creation Science Association. In the 34 years since that time he has served as president, secretary and treasurer, and is now president *emeritus* of TCCSA.

Jerry D. Roth is a retired electrical technician who worked for Honeywell Inc. for 31 years as an investigative analyst of vendor component defects.

After graduating from High School he served in the U.S. Army for three years with the Headquarters Army Security Agency in Tokyo, Japan. Following his Army duty he attended William Hood Dunwoody Industrial Institute and graduated from a course in electronics. Because of an interest in geology he enrolled in extension courses at the University of Minnesota in Physical Geology, Historical Geology, Geology in National Parks and Isotope Geology (radiometric dating). Geology field trip participation included trips in the United States, Canada and Europe.

He served as president of the Twin Cities Creation Science Association for 6 years, having been involved with the organization for 22 years. He currently resides in Tennessee, and is now with East Tennessee Creation Science Association.

His main hobbies are archery, hunting for deer and elk and flying a small home-built airplane.